FINDING THE
WILD WEST:
THE PACIFIC WEST

FINDING THE
WILD WEST:
THE PACIFIC WEST

CALIFORNIA, OREGON, IDAHO, WASHINGTON, AND ALASKA

MIKE COX

TWODOT®

ESSEX, CONNECTICUT
HELENA, MONTANA

A · TWODOT® · BOOK

An imprint and registered trademark of Globe Pequot, the trade division of
The Rowman & Littlefield Publishing Group, Inc.
4501 Forbes Blvd., Ste. 200
Lanham, MD 20706
www.rowman.com

Distributed by NATIONAL BOOK NETWORK

British Library Cataloguing in Publication Information available

Library of Congress Cataloging-in-Publication Data

Names: Cox, Mike, 1948- author.
Title: Finding the Wild West. The Pacific West. : California, Oregon,
    Idaho, Washington, and Alaska / Mike Cox.
Other titles: Pacific West : California, Oregon, Idaho, Washington, and
    Alaska
Description: Essex, Connecticut : TwoDot, [2022] | Series: Finding the Wild
    West series | Includes index.
Identifiers: LCCN 2022026716 (print) | LCCN 2022026717 (ebook) | ISBN
    9781493064175 (paperback) | ISBN 9781493064182 (epub)
Subjects: LCSH: Historic sites—Pacific States—Guidebooks. | Historic
    sites—West (U.S.)—Guidebooks. | Historic sites—Alaska—Guidebooks. |
    Pacific States—History—19th century. | West (U.S.)—History—19th
    century. | Alaska—History—19th century. | Overland journeys to the
    Pacific—History.
Classification: LCC F852.3 .C69 2022 (print) | LCC F852.3 (ebook) | DDC
    287.09465—dc23/eng/20220623
LC record available at https://lccn.loc.gov/2022026716
LC ebook record available at https://lccn.loc.gov/2022026717

♾™ The paper used in this publication meets the minimum requirements of American
National Standard for Information Sciences—Permanence of Paper for Printed Library
Materials, ANSI/NISO Z39.48-1992.

Writers typically dedicate their books to a particular person, but this book is dedicated to a singularly spiritual moment in the once Wild West and the three people who shared it with me. On June 20, 2016, on our way to the annual Western Writers of America conference, Beverly Waak and I, along with our friends Preston and Harriet Lewis, visited the Little Bighorn Battlefield National Monument. In this historic place where two cultures collided so violently, what we perceived, lingering over the still-remote landscape like traces of gun smoke, was an overwhelming sense of peace. At the circular memorial commissioned by the Lakota to honor their fallen warriors, I happened to look up into a dark blue Montana sky. Having traveled to a lot of places over many decades, I had never seen anything like this: a long, high, thin cloud that looked very much like a giant eagle feather. Beverly, Harriet, and Preston saw it, too. Freak of weather? Somehow, it didn't feel like that. Rather, it was as if the sky, in concert with the wind and the sun, wanted to remind us with its rendering of such a sacred American Indian icon that no matter what, all of us are connected—to each other, to the past, and to the land.

—Mike Cox

CONTENTS

Oregon

Idaho

PREFACE: FINDING THE WILD WEST

Ain't nothing better than riding a fine horse in a new country.
—GUS MCCREA IN *LONESOME DOVE*

LIKE MOST BABY BOOMERS, I LEARNED ABOUT THE OLD WEST IN the mid-1950s and early 1960s watching black-and-white television westerns and John Wayne movies in color. But that was Hollywood's Old West.

Thanks largely to my late granddad, L.A. Wilke, I began to learn about the real Old West. He was born in Central Texas in the fading days of that era, just long enough ago to have learned how to ride a horse well before he ever got behind the wheel of an automobile. Too, as a youngster and later as a newspaperman, he met some notable Wild West figures, from Buffalo Bill Cody to old Texas Rangers who had fought Comanches. A fine storyteller, he shared his experiences with me. Also, he passed his copies of *True West* and *Frontier Times* on to me. At the time, his friend Joe Small published both magazines in Austin, where I grew up.

Even before I started reading nonfiction Western magazines and books, again thanks to Granddad, I got to visit some Old West historic sites when they were still just abandoned ruins. With him, as a first grader I prowled around old Fort Davis in West Texas well before the federal government stabilized it as a National Historic Site. Later, Granddad took me to several southwest New Mexico ghost towns, including Shakespeare, Hillsboro, and Kingston. This was in 1964, when many of that state's roadways were not yet paved. In that desert high country, I experienced for the first time the still-vast openness of the West and the sense of adventure in exploring an old place new to me.

So why was the West wild?

I think you will come to understand the "why" when you experience the "where" of the Wild West. Though many of the sites described in these books are in populated areas, some are as remote, or more remote, than they were back in the Wild West's heyday. In visiting these sites—say, a ghost town well off the beaten path—you should be able to feel the reason why the West was wild. When I stand in the middle of nowhere, distant from nothing, I feel the sense of freedom that must have driven so much of human behavior in frontier times. In such emptiness, usually scenic, it's easy to believe you can do anything you, by God, want to, be it bad or good.

Some see the West as being all the states west of the Mississippi, which includes twenty-three states. Others maintain that the West begins at the ninety-eighth meridian. My belief is that the Mississippi River is what separates the East from the West in the US.

Accordingly, moving from east to west, this series of travel guides divides the West into five regions: along the Mississippi (Louisiana, Arkansas, Iowa, Minnesota, and Missouri); the Great Plains (Oklahoma, Kansas, Nebraska, South Dakota, and North Dakota); the Southwest (Arizona, New Mexico, and Texas); the Mountain West (Colorado, Montana, Nevada, Utah, and Wyoming); and the Pacific West (Alaska, California, Idaho, Oregon, and Washington).

Having described what I consider the West, what constitutes "wild"?

Former Wild West History Association president Robert G. (Bob) McCubbin, a history buff who acquired one of the world's most inclusive collections of Western photographs, ephemera, books, and artifacts, a few years back offered his take on the matter.

"The Wild West was a time and place unique in the history of the world," he wrote. "It took place on the plains, prairies, mountains, and deserts of the American West, from the Mississippi River to the

Pacific Ocean. It began about the time of the California gold rush and was at its height in the 1870s through the 1890s, fading away in the decade after the turn of the twentieth century—as the automobile replaced the horse."

He went on to explain that Wild West does not mean wilderness wild. It means lawless wild. While untamed grandeur was certainly a part of the Wild West, it was the untamed men and women who made the West wild.

"Of course," McCubbin continued, "during the Wild West period there were many good and substantial citizens who went about their business in a law abiding and constructive way. Most of those are forgotten. It's the excitement of the Wild West's bad men, desperadoes, outlaws, gunfighters, and lawmen—many of whom were also, at times, cowboys, scouts, and buffalo hunters—and the dance hall girls and 'shady ladies,' who capture our interest and imagination."

While mostly adhering to McCubbin's definition of the Wild West, I could not stick to it entirely. Some things that happened prior to the California gold rush—Spanish and French colonial efforts, the Louisiana Purchase, the Lewis and Clark Expedition, the exploits of mountain men, the development of the great western trails, and the Mexican War of 1846 to 1848—were critical in shaping the later history of the West. That explains why some of the sites associated with these aspects of history needed to be included in this book.

For the most part, 1900 is the cut-off date for events related in this series of books. But the Wild West did not end at 11:59 p.m. on December 31, 1899. Some places, particularly Arizona, Oklahoma, New Mexico, and far west Texas, stayed wild until World War I. Sometimes, events that occurred in the nineteenth century continued to have ramifications in the early twentieth century. An example would be the life and times of Pat Garrett, who killed Billy the Kid in 1881. Garrett himself was shot to death in 1909, so his death site is listed.

The Finding the Wild West series is not intended as a guide to every single historic site in a given city, state, or region. Some towns and cities had to be left out. It would take an encyclopedic, multi-volume work to cover *all* the historical places throughout the western states. I have tried to include the major sites with a Wild West connection, along with some places with great stories you've probably never heard.

These books focus primarily on locations where there is still something to see today. Those sites range from period buildings and ruins to battlefields, historical markers, tombstones, and public art. In addition to historic sites, I have included museums and libraries with collections centered on "those thrilling days of yesteryear." Again, I have *not* listed every museum or every attraction.

A note on directions: Since almost everyone has access to GPS applications or devices, locations are limited to specific addresses with "turn here" or "until you come to" used only when necessary, with the exception of block-row-plot numbers of graves (when available). GPS coordinates are given for more difficult to find locations.

The Wild West has long since been tamed, with nationally franchised fast-food places and big-box stores standing where the buffalo roamed and the deer and the antelope played. Considered another way, however, the Wild West hasn't gone anywhere. It still exists in our collective imagination—a mixture of truth and legend set against the backdrop of one of the world's most spectacular landscapes.

Wild Bill Hickok, Jesse James, George Armstrong Custer, Billy the Kid, Wyatt Earp, and others received a lot of press and rose from the dead as Western icons, but there were many more characters—from outlaws to lawmen, drovers to cattle barons, harlots to preachers—whose stories are yet to be brought to life. Indeed, every tombstone, every historical marker, every monument, every ghost town, every historic site, every place name, every structure, every person has a story to tell. Like a modern-day prospector, all you need to do is pack these books in your saddlebag, mount up, and ride out in search of the Wild West.

—Mike Cox
Wimberley, Texas

INTRODUCTION: THE PACIFIC WEST

The settling of the American West began at its far eastern edge along the Mississippi River, and, on its western edge, along the Pacific Ocean. The vast land in between would later be filled from both sides.

In 1769, in what would become California, Spain began establishing a series of twenty-one missions intended to convert American Indians to Christianity. To protect these missions the empire also built four presidios. The European empire claimed the land all the way up the coastline to future Washington, but it never tried to extend its footprint very far beyond San Francisco Bay. One of the reasons for that was the existence farther up the coast of a Russian colonial trading post that continued in operation until the early 1840s.

When Mexico won its independence from Spain in 1821, the new republic split California into two provinces: Alta California on the north, and Baja California on the south.

In 1848, following Mexico's defeat in its war with the United States, Mexico ceded a huge amount of land to America, including Alta California. Soon after, Americans discovered gold in the northern mountains of the new US territory, and Congress quickly granted California statehood in 1850.

Although what would become Washington had been visited in the late 1700s by both British and US seafarers, the first Euro-Americans to reach the area on the ground were explorers Meriwether Lewis and William Clark in 1805. Beginning in 1810, both Britain and the United States established trading posts in what would become Washington and Oregon, areas rich in wildlife and timber. In fact,

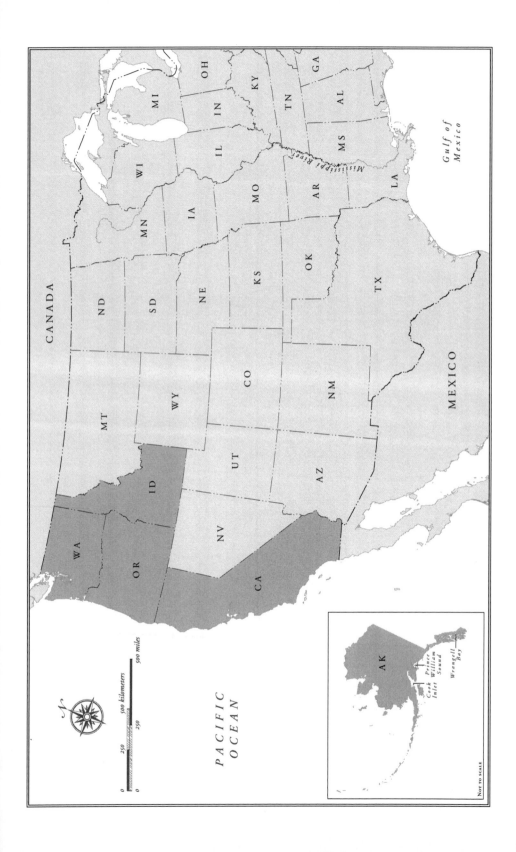

Great Britain did not relinquish its claim to the Northwest until 1846, when the 49th parallel was established as the southern boundary of British territory.

The land between the 49th parallel and the California border was designated as Oregon Territory in 1848. In 1853, Congress cut the territory in half, creating Washington Territory from the northern portion. Oregon became a state in 1859, but Washington was not admitted to the Union until 1888.

What is now Idaho was originally part of Oregon Territory, but after Oregon statehood the land area that would become Idaho was inside the boundaries of Washington Territory. In 1863, Congress created Idaho Territory, its western border set as the state of Oregon and Washington Territory, its eastern border extending to the western boundaries of Dakota and Nebraska Territories. For a time that made Idaho the largest of the nation's ten territories, its land then including all of what would become the states of Montana and Wyoming. But when Idaho achieved statehood in 1890, its eastern border was pulled back to create its permanent configuration.

The last Pacific land acquired by the United States was Alaska, which it purchased from Russia in 1867. Many saw the acquisition of Alaska as a waste of taxpayer money—until the Yukon gold discovery in 1897. Finally designated a territory in 1912, Alaska became the forty-ninth state in 1959.

The addition of Alaska meant that two of the nation's three largest states were in the Pacific West. Alaska is the largest of the fifty, with California ranking third. Texas completes the triad as the second-largest state.

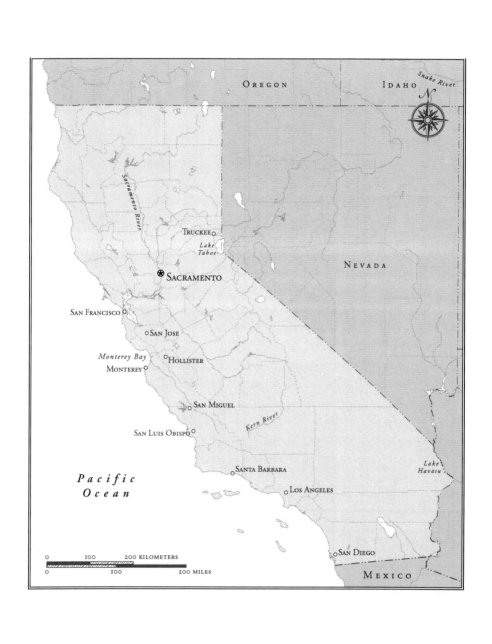

CALIFORNIA

AMADOR CITY (AMADOR COUNTY)

Since "city" means a large town, referring to this old gold-mining community in the western foothills of the Sierra Nevada as Amador City is something of a stretch. It's small (in fact, it's California's least-populated incorporated city), but definitely not a ghost town. Named for prosperous California rancher José Maria Amador, who in 1848 began placer mining along the creek that also bears his name, the town was founded in 1851. Two years later, Amador City's best-known mine, the Keystone, opened. In operation from 1853 to 1942, it produced $24 million in gold. When the mine closed, the town went into decline. But beginning in the 1960s, Amador City found a new form of "gold"—wineries and heritage tourism.

A walking tour available from the **Amador County Chamber of Commerce** (70 Ridge Rd., Sutter Creek; 209-223-0350) points out fifteen historic buildings and locations associated with Amador City's boom days. One of the more notable structures is the redbrick, two-story **Imperial Hotel** (14202 Old State Highway 49; 209-267-9172). Built in 1879, it continues to host overnight guests.

Directly behind the hotel, the town's permanent residents lie in **Amador City Cemetery**. Markers in the 1.25-acre cemetery allow visitors to take a self-guided tour of interesting graves.

Located in the 1860 Kling Building—the town's oldest commercial structure—is the **Amador Whitney Museum** (209-267-5250). Used for a time as the local office of Wells Fargo, by the early 1990s the building was owned by antiques dealer Jerrold Whitney and artist Clayton Pinkerton. In their wills, they bequeathed the building to the town for use as a museum, hence its name. The museum opened in 1993.

Also in Amador City is the **Western Hardrock Mining Museum** (14207 Old State Highway 49; 209-267-0848). Located in an antiques store, the museum has a large collection of vintage mining equipment and gold rush memorabilia.

The Volcano that Wasn't

One of the best-preserved and least touristy ghost towns in Amador County is Volcano. The community dates to 1848, when a group of ex-soldiers who had served during the just-ended Mexican-American War found gold in the area. The men had survived combat, and had proved to be adept prospectors, but they didn't know nearly as much about geology as they thought.

Noting that the gulch where they'd discovered placer gold lay in the middle of a bowl-shaped formation, the recently discharged soldiers assumed they had stumbled on the remnants of an ancient volcano, and thought that sounded like a good name for the new mining camp. Compounding their error, they further believed that the multihued stone they found in the area was lava.

The miners' geological theory was in time disproven, but the name Volcano stuck. While their knowledge of vulcanism was skewed, the prospectors hadn't been wrong in their belief that a lot of gold was going to be extracted from the area. Volcano erupted as a mining boomtown, with as many as five thousand residents, and money continued to spew forth until the amount of precious metal being found waned in the mid-1860s.

The old town's most notable survivor of the gold-mining era is the **St. George Hotel**, a three-story brick structure built in the early to mid-1860s. It still accommodates overnight guests. Other buildings include an old jail dating to 1871; the former Sing Kee Store, which included the local Adams Express Agency (the forerunner of Wells Fargo) office; the two-story frame Union Hotel (which included a saloon and billiards tables), and other complete and partial structures. To reach Volcano, take State Highway 88 from Jackson to Pine Grove, then turn left on Volcano Road. The town is a little over three miles from the highway turnoff.

ANGELS CAMP (CALAVERAS COUNTY)

The heavenly sounding name of this town, founded in 1849 during the California Gold Rush, did not mean its residents sported wings and halos. In fact, two of California's most notorious outlaws spent time around here—Joaquin Murrieta and Black Bart. The town's angelic name came from George Angel, who established a mining camp and trading post. More than $100 million in gold was extracted in the vicinity before the lode petered out.

The **Angels Camp Museum** (753 South Main St.; 209-736-2963) covers three acres and features an assortment of restored or re-created Gold Rush–era buildings. With 30,000 square feet of exhibit space, the museum complex covers all aspects of the area's Gold Rush history and features one of the nation's largest collections of vintage wagons and carriages.

The **Angels Hotel** (Main Street and Bird Way) started as a canvas tent put up by C. C. Lake in 1851. As the mining camp boomed, a one-story frame building replaced the tent. A stone building went up in 1855, and two years later a second floor was added. Newspaperman Samuel Clemens (soon to be much better known as Mark Twain) was a hotel guest in 1865 when he first heard from a bartender the tale that he would transform into a short story called "The Celebrated Jumping Frog of Calaveras County." (The Angels Camp Museum has an exhibit on Twain and his famous short story.) Listed on the National Register of Historic Places, the old building is no longer a hotel, but the annual Jumping Frog Jubilee jumping frog contest takes place on the sidewalk in front of it.

AUBURN (PLACER COUNTY)

Camping in the foothills of the Sierra Nevada Mountains northwest of Sacramento—on their way to the newly found gold bonanza at Coloma, discovered on May 16, 1848—three Frenchmen realized they needn't go any farther. They had stumbled on their own rich vein of gold, only the third find in California's Mother Lode. First known as "North Fork Dry Diggings," the suddenly booming mining town was named Auburn in 1849. Following Placer County's organization in 1851, Auburn became the county seat. Its economic engine further stoked by the arrival of the railroad in the 1860s, Auburn flourished until the gold played out.

Opened in 1994, the **Placer County Museum** (101 Maple St.; 530-889-6500) occupies the ground floor of the three-story, granite-and-brick Placer County courthouse, built in 1898 and still in use. The museum covers the county's early American Indian inhabitants and the Gold Rush era. A self-guided walking tour of Auburn historic sites is also available through the museum.

The Pirate of the Placers

The son of a British army officer, Richard A. Barter grew up in Canada, but like so many others, he came to the Northern California gold country in 1850 hoping to cash in on the new Eldorado. Settling at a mining camp on the North Fork of the American River, known as Rattlesnake Bar, Barter acquired his nickname—Rattlesnake Dick.

The name made Barter sound more ominous than he was—at least, at first. He dodged jail time after being accused of purloining clothes from a Jewish peddler, but stealing a mule netted him a one-way trip to San Quentin Prison. There he met a convict named Tom Hughes. After escaping from San Quentin, now calling himself Tom Bell, Hughes organized an outlaw gang with as many as thirty members. After completing his sentence, Barter joined Bell and his colleagues in robbing gold-laden pack trains or stagecoaches. When Bell finally got caught—and hanged—by vigilantes, Barter formed his own criminal cabal and took up where Bell had left off. Soon Rattlesnake Dick, who began using the alias of Dick Wood, became better known as the Pirate of the Placers.

Auburn constable John Boggs relentlessly pursued Rattlesnake Dick and the gang. Finding the outlaw and several of his cohorts a mile south of Auburn on July 11, 1859, Boggs's attempt to make arrests devolved into a gun battle that left one deputy dead and another wounded. Boggs believed Rattlesnake Dick had been wounded, but the bandit escaped.

The lawman had been right. Badly wounded, Rattlesnake Dick opted to kill himself. When they found him the next morning, the dead outlaw gripped a revolver in his right hand and clutched a piece of paper in the other. Written in pencil, one side of the paper read: "Rattlesnake Dick dies but never surrenders, as all true Britons do."

They buried Rattlesnake Dick twice. His first grave was in the Old Auburn District Cemetery. But in 1893 his remains were exhumed and reburied in Auburn's new city cemetery (1040 Collins Dr.). A large, irregular granite slab placed in the twentieth century marks his grave.

BODIE (MONO COUNTY)

Reverend F. M. Warrington arrived in Bodie in 1861 to find a town with no shortage of work for a preacher, even if a lot of it involved conducting funerals. With its sixty-five saloons (not to mention brothels and gambling places), Warrington saw Bodie as "a sea of sin, lashed by the tempests of lust and passion." Like so many other early California towns, it was the lust for gold, not necessarily the pleasures of the flesh, that led to Bodie's founding in 1859, when good diggings were discovered in the area by Waterman S. Bodey (also spelled "Body"), who gave the mining camp its name, if not its exact spelling.

After production at the most significant mine in the vicinity declined, so did Bodie. But the town gained new life when a cave-in exposed a new rich vein of ore in 1870. By 1876, Bodie had a population of ten thousand and a deserved reputation for roughness. Legend holds that one man a day died violently. "Good-bye, God! We are moving to Bodie!" a young girl was said to have written in her diary when she learned her family planned on moving to the wild boomtown. Production from the mines began to wane in the first half of the 1880s, and a devastating fire in 1892 set the town back even further.

When people began leaving Bodie by the figurative ore wagonload, they left the town intact. In 1929, the ghost town attracted the attention of Universal Studies, which briefly brought the town back to life while filming the Western *Hell's Heroes*. In that film, Bodie starred as New Jerusalem, a fictional New Mexico town. While the studio was only interested in saving money by not having to build a substantial Western town set, the movie proved to be a gift to posterity. In 1932, another fire destroyed 70 percent of the town. Fortunately, Bodie's pre-fire appearance had been captured on camera. Despite the fragility of early nitrate film, the movie has survived. Though flames claimed many of its old buildings, the town's remote location and high altitude (8,000-plus feet above sea level) left it better preserved than most abandoned mining boomtowns. When the state opened the site as **Bodie State Historic Park** (seven miles south of Bridgeport at the end of State Road 270; 760-616-5040) in 1962, nearly 170 of its original wooden buildings still stood. The state maintains the site in what the park's website calls "arrested decay." That means Bodie still looks like an old mining town, not a reconstructed old mining town. The park is open only during daylight hours, with no facilities other than drinking water and toilets.

BORREGO SPRINGS (SAN DIEGO COUNTY)

A small town surrounded by a vast desert, Borrego Springs is not noted for anyone who ever lived here or for anything that ever happened here, but for the multiple thousands of west-bound travelers who passed through the area in the middle nineteenth century.

The last leg of the east–west transportation route known as the Southern Emigrant Trail cut through the desert in what is now eastern San Diego County. A long segment of the old trail can be explored in **Anza-Borrego Desert State Park** (200 Palm Canyon Dr.; 760-767-4205). The name honors Spanish explorer Captain Juan Bautista de Anza, whose command passed through this desert while blazing a south-to-north trail from Sonora (in what is now Mexico) to San Francisco, in 1774. The second part of the name is the Spanish word for sheep, for the bighorn sheep found in the bordering high country.

The Southern Emigrant Trail, much of it following trails developed by American Indians, was first used by whites during the Mexican-American War when Lieutenant Philip St. George Cooke's command traveled across this part of California on their way to San Diego in 1847. Following the discovery of gold in Northern California, thousands of Forty-Niners made their way through this desert. Later, the Butterfield Overland Mail used the same trail.

In addition to maps and general informational material, the Anza-Borrego Desert State Park visitor center has exhibits interpreting the history of the area and the trail that passed through it. California's largest recreation area, the park covers more than a half-million acres.

CALICO (SAN BERNARDINO COUNTY)

The quest for silver, not gold, led to the founding of this town in the middle of the Mojave Desert. During its heyday in the 1880s, Calico had some 3,500 residents with 500 mines operating in the Calico Mining District. But when the price of silver plummeted in 1893, so did Calico's fortunes. At its peak, Calico had been producing 10 percent of the nation's silver. Considered one of the best-preserved ghost towns in the nation, all but five of its buildings were restored in the early 1950s by Walter Knott of Knott's Berry Farm fame. His uncle had been county sheriff during the town's wild and woolly days. In 1966, the Knott family deeded the town site to the county, which operates it as **Calico Ghost Town Regional Park** (36600 Ghost Town Rd.; 760-254-3679), four miles northwest of Yermo. An 1887-vintage adobe building on Main Street known as the **Lane House** opened as a museum in 2001.

CAMPO (SAN DIEGO COUNTY)

Only two miles north of the Mexican border, the community of Campo began in 1868, when brothers Silas and Lumen (some sources have his name as "Luman") Gaskill arrived from Northern California to open a general store. In addition, they built a hotel, a gristmill, and a blacksmith shop. Their customers were primarily area ranchers, many having come to California from Texas following the Civil War. In fact, for a time the area was informally known as "Little Texas."

The Gaskills did well, also enjoying trade with people who patronized the store from south of the border. At midmorning on December 4, 1875, however, it was trouble that came up from Mexico. Bandits rode into town to plunder the store, but the Gaskills and others opened fire on them. According to some sources, the shoot-out that followed is reputed to be second only to the infamous 1881 gunfight at the O.K. Corral in Tombstone, Arizona, in terms of duration, shots fired, and lives lost, although there were many livelier (and actually, deadlier) gunfights elsewhere in the Wild West. Still, when the black-powder smoke cleared, a sheepherder known only as Frenchy lay dead, and Lumen Gaskill was gravely wounded. Also seriously wounded (having been shot by Frenchy before he died), the leader of the gang died a year later. Two raiders escaped uninjured but were soon captured. However, not long after they were locked up they were freed from jail by unknown parties—and lynched.

The original Gaskill store was replaced by a more substantial stone building in 1885. The Gaskills continued to operate their store, and also ran a ranch, until they moved to San Diego in 1902. The old mercantile building now is home to the **Gaskill Stone Store Museum** (31130 State Highway 94; 619-663-1885). Operated by the Mountain Empire Historical Society, the museum tells the story of the gunfight.

The Last Horse Soldiers

In John Ford's classic 1939 western, *Stagecoach*, the passengers of a stagecoach being attacked by Indians are saved at the last minute as a company of US Cavalry—bugles blaring, guidons flying, raised sabers flashing—comes galloping to their rescue. From the 1830s through the days of unrest along the border during the Mexican Revolution, the horse soldier was always part of the story.

That's what makes what happened at Campo in 1944 a singular moment in the long story of American westward expansion, even though it occurred well into the twentieth century.

Established just before the beginning of World War II, **Camp Lucket** would have a distinction no one considered at the time: It would be the last cavalry post in the West. From 1941 to 1944, the Eleventh Cavalry Regiment, followed by the all-black Tenth Cavalry Regiment, patrolled the border here to guard remote but militarily vital railroad tracks, tunnels, communication lines, and electric infrastructure when the United States was concerned about possible sabotage, or even invasion.

When it became clear that none of that would be happening, in 1944 the Tenth Regiment was sent to Africa—but their horses stayed behind. This marked the end of an era, well beyond the point most people believe it had already ended.

What's left of the old military installation is now privately owned. A state historical marker points out the site's significance as the place where the Wild West arguably ended.

Coalinga (Fresno County)

Steam locomotives needed freshwater and the bituminous coal it took to heat it. When the Southern Pacific Railroad came through the San Joaquin Valley in 1888, it built a coaling facility along its track here. The railroad unglamorously called it Coaling Station A. Eventually a community developed around the station, and when a post office was established in 1899, Coaling Station A was compacted to the more sonorous Coalinga. Incorporation followed in 1906.

Ruthless Outlaw or Robin Hood?

Joaquin Murrieta was either a ruthless outlaw or a Mexican Robin Hood, out to avenge mistreatment by Anglo Californians. He was one person, five persons, or a composite.

Beyond the mythology, a few facts exist. Whether one person or five, someone was doing a lot of stealing, robbing, and killing in the gold country. To mitigate that, on May 11, 1853, Governor John Bigler signed a legislative act creating the California State Rangers. A former Texas Ranger, Harry Love, was placed in command of the twenty-man body. (Interestingly, although the California Rangers were clearly modeled after the Texas Rangers, in the Lone Star State the Rangers would not have law enforcement authority until the 1870s. They were Indian fighters in Texas.)

The California lawmen would be paid $150 a month for three months, their specific assignment to find five men whose first name was "Joaquin," one of them being "Joaquin Muriata." ("Murrieta" is the most common spelling.) As further incentive, if successful, the rangers would share a $1,000 reward the governor had posted for any one of the Joaquins.

On July 25, 1853, Captain Love and some of his men found an armed party of Mexicans about fifty miles from Monterey. In the fight that followed, the rangers killed two men. One was thought to be Murrieta, the other, his almost equally notorious associate, Three-Fingered Jack. To support their claim that they had eliminated California's most dreaded outlaw and one of his henchmen, the rangers cut off Jack's hand and Murrieta's head. With both specimens preserved in an alcohol-filled jar, the rangers collected their reward.

That the jars with their grisly contents were afterward displayed around the state is factual. Whether the pickled body parts came from the wanted men is still disputed. The head ended up in San Francisco, where it was lost in the 1906 San Francisco earthquake and fire. But the legend of Joaquin Murrieta is still alive and well.

A concrete marker with a metal plaque that summarizes the Murrieta story stands at 32400 Dorris Avenue (State Highway 198). The marker, nine miles north of Coalinga, says Murrieta's death site was fourteen miles from the location of the marker. The actual site is on private property, described by the California Office of Historic Preservation only as "three large rocks in foothills SW of Cantua Creek Bridge, . . . 9 mi N of Coalinga."

COLMA (SAN MATEO COUNTY)

They call Colma the "City of Souls." That's because while only a couple of thousand people live here, more than 1.5 million "souls" everlastingly repose here. Colma has sixteen cemeteries, one being the burial place of a man whose very name is synonymous with the Wild West—Wyatt Earp.

Wyatt Earp's funeral was a parting of two eras. One of the Wild West's most famous gunslingers was gone, but two men who would help perpetuate the Western myth were present that day—western movie stars William S. Hart and Tom Mix. The old gambler-lawman's ashes were buried in his wife Josie's family plot. She rejoined him there following her death in 1944. The graves are located in **Jewish Hills of Eternity Cemetery** (1301 El Camino Real; 650-755-4700). From the cemetery gates, head toward a domed mausoleum marked "C. Meyer." Three-fourths of the way down the row is a series of steps marked "Meier." From those steps, Earp's large dark granite headstone is readily apparent.

Even though the town wasn't incorporated until 1924, Colma's story in a way connects to the days of the California Gold Rush, when precious metal meant more to a lot of people than life itself—at least, someone else's life. When San Francisco boomed in the late 1840s and into the next decade, a lot of people died there of disease, in accidents or at the hands of another. Within a generation, San Francisco had twenty-six well-populated cemeteries. What it lacked was any room for continued growth. With cemeteries full, the city, along with private cemetery owners, began looking for someplace to accommodate the dearly departed. To complicate matters further, the state legislature passed a law in 1887 making it illegal to bury anyone outside an established cemetery. As Colma was an easy carriage ride to the southwest from the city, it soon became the growing metropolis's necropolis.

All Hail Emperor Norton

For a man with his credentials—namely, Emperor of the United States and Protector of Mexico—Joshua Norton certainly lies beneath an unpretentious headstone. Norton came to San Francisco in 1849 seeking a fortune, as did thousands of others. Unlike many, he found it. The Brit managed to make a lot of money, but it was gone in less than a decade. And soon, so was he. Whether his transition from wealth to near destitution led to his mental health issues or whether mental health issues led to his catastrophic financial reverse is unknowable, but when he reappeared in San Francisco nine months later, he possessed a document proclaiming him Emperor of the United States.

Most crackpot claimants are ignored or shunned, but San Francisco embraced him. The *San Francisco Bulletin* published a story announcing Norton's ascension, a print shop printed currency for the Empire, and one of the city's better hotels put him up for free. Many agreed with his style of "governance." He abolished Congress, declared the Union no more, and took on additional duties, naming himself Protector of Mexico. Befitting a man of his stature, Norton wore a regal uniform, and San Franciscans treated him respectfully. He ate for free and got the best seats when he attended a theatrical performance. In fact, the audience would stand when he walked in. He continued his work for the people. He proposed a bridge from San Francisco to Oakland, which later happened. He went from humored eccentric to near sainthood when he attacked something residents had come to hate (and still do)—using "Frisco" as a short descriptor of The City, as most locals called it. By royal decree, the emperor forbade the word, and anyone found in violation was subject to a $25 fine.

Norton died on January 8, 1880, after a twenty-year reign. Thirty thousand people turned out for his long funeral procession. Local businessmen furnished a stately rosewood casket and underwrote a funeral befitting a man of his standing. Sadly, at least for those San Franciscans who appreciated a little levity, the Emperor had not selected a successor.

Norton is buried in **Woodlawn Cemetery** (1000 El Camino Real; 650-755-1727).

COLOMA (EL DORADO COUNTY)

A carriage maker by trade, all New Jersey–born James Marshall knew about gold was that it was shiny and valuable. But on January 24, 1848, purely by accident, he made a discovery that changed US history. Marshall was building a mill for Swiss emigrant John Sutter, who in 1841 had established a colony he called New Helvetia, along the American River in the Sacramento Valley of Northern California. Looking at the water rushing through the millrace he and his men had just completed, he saw a bright particle he later described as being "half the size and the shape of a pea." That, he continued, "made my heart thump, for I was certain it was gold." Indeed, it was gold. As word of the find began to spread, it triggered what remains the largest voluntary mass movement of people in the history of the Western hemisphere.

Coloma became the Wild West's first boomtown. With two thousand prospectors working claims along the river, it soon boasted a population of four thousand.

The centerpiece of the 500-acre **Marshall Gold Discovery State Historic Park** (310 Back St.; 530-622-3470) is a working replica of the mill Marshall built for Sutter. Next to the mill is a reconstructed building, the so-called Mormon cabin, where workers lived during construction of the mill. From there, a trail leads to a monument commemorating Marshall and his discovery. When he died in 1885, at his request he was buried on a hill overlooking Coloma, and the monument stands at his grave. The bronze of Marshall shows him pointing to where he found gold. Across State Highway 49 from the mill site is **Marshall Gold Discovery Museum**. Its exhibits cover the history of the mill and the accidental discovery of gold nearby. Artifacts from an archaeological dig conducted at the site in the 1920s, including some of the original timbers from the mill, are also displayed. The park is eight miles north of Placerville, off State Highway 49.

COLTON (SAN BERNARDINO COUNTY)

The first settlement in this area came in the early 1800s with the establishment of Mission San Gabriel, northeast of the future Colton. After Mexico forcibly separated itself from Spain in 1821, ranching began on a land grant issued by the Mexican government. While ranching and citrus growing continued after California entered the Union, the town of Colton dates from the arrival of the Southern Pacific Railroad in 1875. Named for Southern Pacific vice president David Douty Colton, the community went on to become a busy railroad crossroad.

Virgil Earp came to Colton after the O.K. Corral gunfight to recuperate from the attempt on his life that left him crippled in one arm. In 1887, his reputation overriding his disability, he was elected Colton's first town marshal shortly after the community incorporated, and served until March 1889, earning $75 a month. In observance of the 125th anniversary of the Colton Police Department, its officers wore a commemorative star-shaped badge bearing Earp's likeness, with two pointed six-shooters.

Earp and his wife Allie lived at 528 West H Street. Now privately owned, the house still stands. After the 1957 television show about Wyatt Earp made the Earps famous all over again, a nonprofit group started a three-day event called Wyatt Earp Old West Days, held annually in October. With plans to restore the old house and open it to the public, the group nearly closed on purchasing it, but the owner at the time backed out of the deal. The annual event is no longer held.

Following Morgan Earp's March 18, 1882, assassination in Tombstone, Arizona, his brothers escorted his body to Colton for burial. Doc Holliday furnished the suit they buried him in. Morgan Earp (1851–1882) was first buried in the old Colton cemetery, but in 1892 his remains were exhumed and laid to rest in the **Hermosa Memorial Cemetery** (900 North Meridian Ave.) The Colton Police Department placed a second marker at his grave in 2013.

Housed in the neoclassical former Carnegie Public Library, built in 1908 and used until 1984, the Colton Historical Society opened the **Colton Area Museum** (380 North La Cadena Ave.; 909-824-8814) in 1991. Of particular interest to Wild West history buffs, the museum has a collection of Earp family artifacts, documents, and photographs.

COLUMBIA (TUOLUMNE COUNTY)

The camp that grew near the location of Dr. Thaddeus Hildreth's gold discovery of March 27, 1850, was first known as Hildreth's Diggings, but given the amazing amount of gold being found in the vicinity, a grander, more sweeping name seemed in order, and the boomtown became Columbia. Suddenly ranking as California's second-largest city, for a time Columbia—dubbed the "Gem of the Southern Mines"—was even in the running to become state capital. Sacramento, however, prevailed by two votes. Though the city survived two major fires, in 1854 and 1857, Columbia began to decline in 1860 after its rich placer deposits were exhausted. Still, its post office remained open, and it never became a ghost town. In its heyday, Columbia produced some $87 million in gold at mid-nineteenth-century values.

A Lynching with a Twist

Lynchings were almost as common as picks and shovels in Northern California during the early Gold Rush days, but the hanging-by-committee of John S. Barclay had a couple of unusual variations. The first thing that made it atypical was the fact that local miners would have even bothered to string him up. After all, when Barclay shot and killed John H. Smith in a saloon, he did it to protect his wife.

On October 10, 1855, well in his cups, Smith dropped and broke a pitcher. Proprietress Maggie Barclay ordered him out of her place of business with a barrage of profanity. Smith pushed her hard and she fell into a chair just as her husband walked into the bar. Thinking to defend his wife, John Barclay pulled his revolver and put a bullet in Smith.

Local law enforcement did not see that as a chivalrous act and arrested him for murder. Unfortunately for Barclay, Smith had a lot of friends in town. One was J. W. Coffroth, a lawyer with all the good persuasive skills expected of a successful attorney. However, his exhortations resulted in a mob forcibly removing Barclay from jail, trying him (with Coffroth as prosecutor and the local newspaper editor as his nominal defense counsel), and finally, in the defendant being strung up from an overhead sluice. The second unusual thing about the lynching was that in their frenzy, the vigilance committee had overlooked tying Barclay's hands. Fighting for his life, Barclay pulled up on the rope and kept the pressure off his neck—at least until his grip finally failed.

John H. Smith (1803–1855) lies in what is now known as the Columbia Public Cemetery beneath a wooden cross with only his name carved across it. Barclay's grave is not marked. The cemetery—actually, three connected cemeteries—is located at the end of School House Road, on the edge of the town.

With the centennial of the Gold Rush approaching, California purchased most of the town in 1945 and began maintaining it as the **Columbia State Historic Site** (11255 Jackson St.; 209-588-9128). Three miles north of Sonora, Columbia is considered the best preserved of the old Northern California mining camps. Among numerous mid-nineteenth-century structures are the 1856 City Hotel and the 1857 Fallon Hotel.

CORONADO (SAN DIEGO COUNTY)

The West had plenty of wild left when in 1885 developers, organized as the Coronado Beach Company, began transforming an old Spanish colonial whaling port across the bay from San Diego into a resort.

Built by two thousand Chinese laborers and opened in 1888, the sprawling five-story, four-hundred-room **Hotel del Coronado** (1500

Orange Ave.) was a Victorian architectural masterpiece, with white siding, balconies, turrets, and a red roof. Still in operation, and now with seven hundred rooms, the hotel has accommodated presidents, Hollywood notables, honeymooners, vacationers, and who knows how many shady characters with sufficient funds to rent a room. Former Tombstone, Arizona, lawman Wyatt Earp and his wife lived in San Diego from about the time construction of the hotel began until 1896, and while there is no documentation, they are said to have spent a night or two at the hotel. It remains the largest frame structure west of the Mississippi.

Though Coronado could be reached by traveling a seven-mile isthmus known as the Silver Strand, the easiest way to reach the resort was by ferry. That held until 1969, when a two-mile-long bridge finally connected it with San Diego.

DANVILLE (CONTRA COSTA COUNTY)

Though the area's settlement dates to a pair of cattle and sheep ranches established on a Mexican land grant called Rancho San Ramon, the San Ramon Valley town of Danville developed in the 1850s as a farming community. The arrival of a Southern Pacific spur route in 1891 made it even easier to get produce to the market, and the town prospered.

Listed on the National Register of Historic Places, the restored former Southern Pacific depot is home to the **Museum of the San Ramon Valley** (205 Railroad St.; 925-837-3750). An hour east of San Francisco, the **Blackhawk Museum** (3700 Blackhawk Plaza Circle; 925-736-2280), a collection of five galleries focused on vintage automobiles, art, technology, and history, features an extensive permanent exhibit called "The Spirit of the Old West." With deference both to American Indians and the Euro-Americans who eventually claimed their land, the exhibit covers the saga of US western expansion from the early 1800s to the beginning of the twentieth century.

Considered one of the best of the West, the exhibit comes with its own interesting history, one that's practically a metaphor for the settlement of the West: Redding, Pennsylvania–born Jerry Fick grew up in a farming family. When as a boy he found a flint spear point on his family's land, he became interested in American Indian and Old West history and went on to acquire a large collection of artifacts representative of the West's original peoples and the culture that followed. In 1989, Fick moved to Cody, Wyoming, where he opened Tecumseh's Frontier Trading Post to showcase his collection. Looking to preserve a lifetime of acquisitions, in 2014 Flick conveyed his collection—which ranges from flint projectile points to vintage Old West firearms—to the Blackhawk Museum.

Death Valley National Park

From the Amargosa Range on the east and the Panamint Range on the west, a 156-mile-long basin cuts diagonally across the Mojave Desert through Nevada into California. With an average annual rainfall of less than two inches, the valley is a land of extremes, with elevations ranging from an 11,049-foot mountain peak to a basin 282 feet below sea level, and temperatures varying by season and altitude from below freezing to a record 134 degrees. Known to American Indians for millennia, this valley was first penetrated by Euro-Americans in 1849, when a lost wagon train of gold seekers moved slowly across it and barely survived the experience.

While only one of the so-called Forty-Niners died, the journey had been so arduous that when they were finally leaving the area, someone supposedly exclaimed "Good-bye, death valley." From then on, the dangerous but decidedly spectacular landscape was known by this enduring name.

In 1881 the mineral borax (used in making soap and other products) was discovered in the valley, and mining soon began. Once the ore was processed, it had to be transported 165 miles to the railhead at Mojave, Utah. This was accomplished by loading the ore into huge wagons with ten-foot-diameter wheels, each one so heavy that it required twenty mules to pull it. Borax mining lasted for less than a decade, but the descriptor "twenty-mule team" would become a Western icon.

In 1933, Congress designated much of the valley as a national monument. The National Park Service used the Depression-era Civilian Conservation Corps to develop what would expand to a 3.33-million-acre **Death Valley National Park**—the largest in the Lower 48.

The Furnace Creek visitor center (760-786-3200) in the small community of Death Valley is on State Highway 190, which cuts through the sprawling park. The visitor center has no specific street address, but the NPS website notes that the address for the nearby Death Valley post office is 328 Greenland Boulevard.

Death Valley Days Radio Show

For a place with such an ominous name, Death Valley gave life to an old-time radio show—and later, a television series—that made "borax" a household word and dramatized true stories of the Old West for more than three decades.

Sponsored by Pacific Coast Borax Company, which produced the 20 Mule Team Borax and Boraxo brands, *Death Valley Days* hit the airwaves in 1930 and ran until 1945. After a seven-year hiatus, the show became a popular television series that lasted from 1952 to 1970.

The first host was Stanley Andrews, identified on the show only as "The Old Ranger." When he left the show in 1964, the nearly forgotten actor who followed him as host (and played a part in twenty-two episodes as well) enjoyed a renewed national exposure that went a long way toward propelling him to the White House. On the show from 1964 to 1965, his name was Ronald Reagan.

After 458 half-hour episodes that influenced how two generations would view the epoch of US western expansion, the series ended its run in 1970.

EARP (SAN BERNARDINO COUNTY)

After Wyatt Earp became even more famous following the release of the highly fictionalized book by Walter Noble Burns, *Tombstone: An Iliad of the Southwest*, the small town of Drennan renamed itself in Earp's honor. The old gambler-gunfighter and his common-law wife Josie Marcus lived in this still-remote area near the California–Arizona border off and on from 1906 to the mid-1920s, as Earp worked his "Happy Days" mine in the Whipple Mountains. From 1925 to 1928, the couple lived in a cottage in nearby Vidal, California. The Earp cottage, marked by a state historical plaque, still stands on Old Park Road, one-tenth of a mile east of US 95, Vidal.

ESCONDIDO (SAN DIEGO COUNTY)

In 1776, Spaniard Juan Bautista de Anza explored the Escondido Valley, but settlement did not begin there until 1843. That year the Republic of Mexico, which had taken control of California in 1821, granted 12,653 acres in the valley to Juan Bautista Alvarado, who named it Rancho Rincon Diablo. The United States acquired California at the end of the 1846–1848 Mexican-American War, but more than four decades passed before the town of Escondido was surveyed and platted, in 1886.

The Old Escondido Historic District includes nearly nine hundred properties, many dating from the city's earliest days. A self-guided tour of the district, which is bounded by Fifth Avenue on the north, 13th Avenue on the south, Escondido Boulevard on the west, and Chestnut Street on the east, can be downloaded from oldescondido.org/tours. Located in the city's first public library, the **Escondido History Center** (321 North Broadway; 760-743-8207) maintains a large local history archive, and has moved four other historic buildings to the site and restored them.

The December 6, 1846, Battle of San Pasqual pitted American troops against Californios, people of Hispanic descent living in California after Mexico gained independence from Spain in 1821. In the battle, Captain Andres Pico and his men were fighting to keep their homeland. The Americans, a force of the First Dragoons under General Stephen W. Kearney, were fighting to fold California into the growing United States. Both sides claimed victory, but more US soldiers (twenty-one) died in the engagement than Californios (one, plus several wounded). The battle was the bloodiest of the Mexican-American War in California.

Just under eight miles southeast of Escondido, the **San Pasqual Battlefield State Park**'s visitor center (15808 San Pasqual Valley Rd.; 760-737-2201) has interpretive exhibits on the circumstances leading to the battle and the Mexican-American War's impact on California and the West.

Five miles west of the park (off Pomerado Road, a tenth of a mile from I-15, San Diego County) is a state historical marker at the site of the **Battle of Mule Hill**. The fight that occurred here happened on December 7, 1846, the day after the battle at San Pasqual. In it, General Kearney's command was besieged by the same Californios they had faced the day before. The high ground on which US forces made their stand was not so named for its resemblance to a mule, but rather because the surrounded dragoons ran low on supplies and were forced to eat some of their mules. Scout Kit Carson and Navy Lieutenant Edward F. Beale managed to slip through enemy lines and ride to San Diego to summon help from Commodore Robert F. Stockton, whose flotilla lay at anchor in San Diego harbor. The commodore dispatched two hundred marines and the Californios broke the siege.

EUREKA (HUMBOLDT COUNTY)

This Northern California city lies just about as far west as a traveler can get. In fact, of US cities of more than 25,000 residents, it's the westernmost of any in the Lower 48.

Eureka was founded on Humboldt Bay—California's second-largest inlet—in 1850, and developed as a supply point for the Mother Lode goldfields. When the precious metal began to be played out, Eureka sustained its economy as a fishing and timber center.

On a bluff overlooking the bay the army established **Fort Humboldt** in 1853 to protect miners and settlers from the native Wiyot people, who were incensed at Euro-American encroachment on their land. The following year an officer who had served during the Mexican-American War, since promoted to captain, was stationed at the fort as a company commander. Not liking the post's isolated location, he resigned his commission. He was Ulysses S. Grant, future Civil War general and US president.

In the spring of 1860, one of many dark moments in Old West history occurred when a vigilante group from Eureka attacked a substantial Wiyot village on what is now known as Indian Island. An estimated 250 men, women, and children were killed in what came to be called the Wiyot Massacre. The military abandoned the fort in 1870 after it was deemed no longer strategically important.

The state acquired the site of the old fort in 1955 and opened it as **Fort Humboldt State Historic Park** (3431 Fort Ave.; 707-445-6547) in 1963. Only one of the post's original fourteen buildings still stands—the old military hospital. The surgeon's quarters that adjoined the hospital, now a museum, was later reconstructed. Founded by high school teacher Cecile Clark in 1960 and located in the old Bank of Eureka building, the **Clarke Historical Museum** (240 E St.; 707-443-1947) focuses on the history of Eureka and northwestern California.

GLENDALE (LOS ANGELES COUNTY)

Only eight years after Spain began establishing missions and presidios in what it called Alta California, in 1784 the governor of the province gave a soldier named Jose Maria Verdugo a land grant of more than 36,000 acres in what is now known as the Los Angeles Basin. The Verdugo family operated a large-scale ranch on the land, later expanding into farming.

In 1828, Verdugo's grandson built an adobe house that still stands, the oldest structure in Glendale. Near the house stand the remnants of a large oak tree, known now as the Oak of Peace. This is where the treaty was negotiated that brought California's involvement in the 1846–1848 Mexican-American War to an early end. The City of Glendale acquired the site in 1989 and maintains it as **Catalina Verdugo Adobe Park** (2211 Bonita Dr.). A historical marker tells more about the 1847 peace treaty.

Verdugo's heirs held their land, known as Rancho San Rafael, through the middle of the nineteenth century, but as California started to develop following statehood, the family began selling off parcels. One of those pieces of land ended up in the hands of real estate developers, who in 1887 began selling lots in a new townsite they named Glendale. The town was incorporated in 1906 and is now part of the metropolitan Los Angeles area.

When he founded **Forest Lawn Memorial Park** (1712 South Glendale Ave.; 888-204-3131) in 1906, Dr. Hubert Eaton envisioned a park-like cemetery so inviting that people would almost look forward to being buried there. He wanted a place "devoid of misshapen monuments and other signs of earthly death, but filled with towering trees, sweeping lawns, splashing fountains, beautiful statuary, and . . . memorial architecture." And that's what he created.

More than 250,000 people are buried in this sprawling, 300-acre cemetery near Hollywood, where at least one million people pass through each year as visitors. Many of the graves belong to former notables, including actors both famous and forgotten, and others in the arts. But the cemetery is also the final resting place of numerous Wild West figures, from sure-enough Old West outlaws and lawmen to chroniclers of the Old West to western film and television stars.

William Ellsworth "Elzy" Lay (1869–1934), who some credit as being the most cunning member of Butch Cassidy's Wild Bunch gang, headed westward from New Mexico's Territorial Prison after receiving a pardon in 1906. Evidently cured of bank and train robbing, he worked as a cowboy before turning to prospecting and then geology. He ended up in the Golden State, where he died of natural causes in Los Angeles. His grave is in Lot 3338 in the Graceland section.

He left his wife Mary buried in Tombstone, Arizona's, Boot Hill Cemetery, but former Tombstone mayor and newspaper publisher John Philip Clum (1851–1932) ended up in greener pastures. Eventually settling in California, he operated a citrus farm and periodically consulted with Hollywood movie producers, offering insight on Apache culture. Lay is buried in Forest Lawn (GPS coordinates: N34° 07.34', W118° 14.72').

Here Lies a Heck of a Marksman

W. Ray Simpson (1862–1940) was running a hardware store in Delta, Colorado, when brothers Tom and Bill McCarty and Bill's son Fred robbed the Farmers and Merchants Bank on September 7, 1893. Hearing all the commotion, Simpson grabbed his old Sharps buffalo rifle and ran outside in time to see the bandits galloping out of town. The shopkeeper took aim and sent a .50 caliber bullet crashing into Bill McCarty's skull. Then Simpson slipped a second cartridge in the rifle and aimed at young Fred McCarty, who wheeled his horse around and fired three shots at the merchant. Fred missed; Simpson did not. With his brother and son lying dead, Tom McCarty succeeded in making it out of town. Simpson is in Crypt 6205 in Glendale's Forest Lawn Memorial Park, Great Mausoleum Sanctuary of Refuge.

One of the twentieth century's most prolific writers of Western fiction, **Louis L'Amour** (1908–1988) is one of Forest Lawn's more noted literary celebrities. L'Amour wrote more than one hundred Western novels, forty-five of which were turned into movies. His novel *Hondo* is listed as one of the 25 Best Western Novels of all time. L'Amour lies in the cemetery's Mausoleum Slope Section, Mausoleum Gardens Division, Private Garden 59.

Forest Lawn is the final resting place of a who's who of western film stars, from pioneer silent movie actors to cowboy crooners to noted film and television performers.

To roll the eternal screen credits, among the faux Westerners buried here are: silent film western star **Art Acord** (1890–1931); **Gilbert M. "Bronco Billy" Anderson** (1880–1971); Dodge City's marshal Matt Dillon, **James Arness** (1923–2011); "Red Ryder" **Donald "Red" Barry** (1912–1980); "Cisco Kid" **Warner Baxter** (1889–1951); B-western star **Johnny Mack Brown** (1904–1974); "Hopalong Cassidy" **William Boyd** (1895–1972); **Victor Daniels** (1899–1955), better known as Chief Thundercloud, and the first Tonto to ride with the Lone Ranger; **Gail Davis** (1925–1997), star of the *Annie Oakley* television series; **Richard Davis** (1886–1946), a Cheyenne better known as Chief Thunderbird; sidekick **George Francis "Gabby" Hayes** (1885–1969); **Alan Ladd** (1913–1964), star of the classic western *Shane*; cowboy actor-singer **Ken Maynard** (1895–1973); **Tom Mix** (1880–1940), buried in the cemetery's Whispering Pines section (1717 South Glendale Ave., lot 1030, space 8); **Frank McGrath** (1903–1967), who played Charlie Wooster in the *Wagon Train* television series; Lone Ranger **Clayton Moore** (1914–1999); **Hugh O'Brian** (1925–2016), who starred as one of the Wild West's more legendary figures in *The Life and Legend of Wyatt Earp*; John Wayne's stunt double **Chuck Roberson** (1919–1988); *F Troop* star **Forrest Tucker** (1919–1986); and perennial bad guy **Lee Van Cleef** (1925–1989).

GRASS VALLEY (NEVADA COUNTY)

Emigrants traveling the Oregon-California Trail needed a lot of equipment and foodstuffs, and places to re-provision were few and far between. They also needed good grazing for their livestock. Fortunately, on the western edge of the Sierra Nevada foothills a stream called Wolf Creek flowed through rich grassland that came to be called Grass Valley. When a mining camp began there in 1849, the town that soon developed there also became Grass Valley.

Grass Valley's downtown has many of its nineteenth-century buildings, including the 1861 **Holbrooke Hotel** (212 Main St.; 530-460-1945). The 1852 Golden Gate Saloon, which has an ornate bar that came by ship around Cape Horn, is part of the hotel. The **Greater Grass Valley Chamber of Commerce and Visitor Center** (228 Main St.; 530-273-4667) offers a self-guided walking tour of the town's historic sites. The **Grass Valley Museum** (410 South Church St.; 530-273-5509) occupies the second floor of the St. Joseph's Cultural Center, a brick former orphanage founded in 1865 by Father William Dalton, pastor of St. Patrick's Church. Orphanages were not uncommon in the Old West, but the focus of this orphanage was different than most. Reflective of the time and place, it took in children who were orphaned by mining accidents.

Grass Valley's Empire Mine was opened in 1850 and continued in operation for more than a century and a half, finally closing in 1956. An estimated 5.8 million ounces of gold came out of the mine, one of the state's oldest and deepest. The old mine, with 367 miles of abandoned shafts, is now the centerpiece of the 856-acre **Empire Mine State Historic Park** (10791 East Empire St.; 530-273-8522).

Whatever Lola Wanted

Lola Montez was already famous when she arrived in California in 1853. Born in Ireland in 1821, her real name was Marie Eliza Gilbert. Her family moved from Ireland to England and then to India. There, she married a British army officer, but that relationship ended. From the British colony she went to Spain to study dance. In 1847, she made her debut in London and soon became a hit, billed as "The Premier Spanish Ballerina." She affected a Spanish accent and adapted "Lola Montez" as a stage name.

While touring Europe, Lola went through a variety of lovers, and for a time was the mistress of the king of Bavaria. Fleeing that country during political unrest in 1848, she came to the United States in 1851. By this point she had transitioned to burlesque, developing a risqué routine she called the Spider Dance. Her act was a spectacular success in the mining camps.

Lola married a newspaper editor and moved with him to Grass Valley in the summer of 1853. When they divorced, she continued to live there until 1855. While in Grass Valley, she mentored a young Lotta Crabtree, teaching her the more respectable aspects of dance. Crabtree went on to have a successful acting career, but Lola's career was in decline. She ended up in Philadelphia, where she died of syphilis in 1861, at the age of thirty-nine.

The original Montez cabin, its life prolonged by a series of renovations, finally had to be torn down in 1975. Someone thought to save Lola's bathtub, which is now on display at the Grass Valley Museum. A reconstruction of the Montez residence was built on the same site (248 Mill St.; 530-273-4667), and now serves as the office for the local chamber of commerce. The house where Crabtree and her family lived still stands at 328 Mill Street, though it has been converted into apartments.

JACKSON (AMADOR COUNTY)

Jackson, founded in 1848 in the heart of the gold-mining country, is the county seat of Amador County. Located seven miles southeast of Amador City, the **Amador County Museum** (225 Church St.; 209-223-6386) focuses on the many old mining camp towns in the county. Among them, in addition to Amador City and Sutter Creek, are Drytown, Fiddletown, Ione, Martell, Plymouth, and Volcano. Other Jackson museum exhibits document the area's American Indian history and the Chinese Americans brought to the area to work in the mines. (Self-guided walking tours of most of these communities are also available from the Amador County Chamber of Commerce in nearby Sutter Creek.)

History buffs interested in getting an even better feel for what the mining life must have been like in the late nineteenth century can take a tour of the 1880 **Kennedy Mine** (1234 Kennedy Mine Rd.; 209-223-9542). One of the deepest gold mines in the world, its shaft descends more than a mile. Before it closed, it produced more than $34 million in gold.

JAMESTOWN (TUOLUMNE COUNTY)

Three and a half miles southwest of Sonora, Jamestown is the town that sprang up after Benjamin F. Woods discovered gold in Tuolumne County in 1848. Originally known as Woods Crossing, the town got its present name from a scoundrel. Of course, no one thought that of George James when he first hit town. He was a gregarious sort, pouring champagne for all and sundry. He made his living, so he said, brokering mining investments. Townspeople were so taken with him that they decided to name the place in James's honor. Unfortunately, James was not worthy of the honor. In truth, he was a con man. Realizing he'd worked about as many suckers as he could, one day he disappeared and was never seen again in the town that bore his name. An engaged citizenry made an effort to change the name, but by that time the Post Office Department had blessed the name and said it could not be changed. Even so, most residents began shortening it to "Jimtown."

Jamestown has buildings dating from the 1850s to the 1890s, including the 1859-vintage **National Hotel** (18183 Main St.; 209-984-3446) and a restored **1897 brick jail** (18201 Main St.), but its primary historical attraction is **Railtown 1897 State Historic Park** (18115 Fifth Ave.; 209-984-3953). From 1897 to 1955, the Sierra Railroad maintained its operational center, general shops, and a roundhouse here. The state of California bought the facility for use as a state park in 1982. Since the first movie was shot here in 1919, when the Sierra Railroad was still a busy line, the well-preserved steam train–era rail yard and its rolling stock—including the much-photographed Sierra Number 3 steam locomotive—has been featured in roughly two hundred films, including the westerns *High Noon* and *Unforgiven*.

JENNER (SONOMA COUNTY)

The Old West might have been considerably wilder if a Tsarist Russian colony in Northern California had succeeded, especially if the European nation had still been around when gold was discovered in the foothills of the Sierra Nevada in 1848. The matter of whether Russia or the United States profited from the bonanza might have triggered conflict, but by then, all of California, soon to become the thirty-first state, was firmly under US control.

While the notion of a nineteenth-century Russia–US conflict is only one of history's many "what-ifs," beginning in 1812 and continuing for nearly thirty years, Russia did have a colony on California's Pacific Coast. It began when California was part of the Spanish empire and continued for much of the time that the Republic of Mexico held sovereignty.

What primarily attracted Russia to North America was the demand for otter furs. The Russians had first established a presence in Alaska, but in 1812, in a business alliance with the young United States, the Russian-American Company built a log outpost in future Sonoma County that came to be called Fortress Ross. (While the name sounds quite American, it's actually derived from *Rossiya*, the Russian word for "Russia.")

Spain, and later, Mexico, were wary of the colony, fearing Russia might try to extend its presence farther south. But at the time, Russia was more interested in commerce and growing crops for shipment to its Alaska settlements, and did not seem land-hungry. In 1841, with most of the otters killed off, and having had little success agriculturally, Russia sold the fort to an American named John Sutter. While his $30,000 purchase (which he never actually paid) marked the end of Russian interest in California, seven years later Sutter would become famous for something else: discovering gold flakes in the American River.

Fort Ross became a state historic park and National Historic Landmark in 1962. Located eleven miles north of Jenner, the 3,400-acre **Fort Ross State Historic Park** (19005 Coast Highway; 707-847-3286) overlooks the Pacific from a broad expanse known as Colony Rock. With no modern development in the area, it looks much as it would have when the imperial Russian flag flew over it.

JULIAN (SAN DIEGO COUNTY)

The gold-mining towns that sprang up in Northern California during the famous 1849 Gold Rush got most of the glory—or infamy. But two decades after the state's first precious metal stampede, Southern California experienced a gold boom centered around Julian.

Located in the Cuyamaca Mountains in eastern San Diego County, Julian was founded after the Civil War by two rebels who headed west, intent on a new start. Cousins Drury Bailey and Mike Julian decided a meadow between Volcan Mountain and the Cuyamacas would be a good place to stop, and that was the beginning of the town named in honor of one of its founders. A freed slave named Fred Coleman found gold in a creek in the winter of 1869, and soon more than eight hundred prospectors converged on the new diggings. A year later, Julian's first gold mine, the Washington Mine, was in operation. Before long, Julian had become San Diego County's second-largest town. Mines in the area produced nearly $2 million in gold over the next thirty years. The **Washington Mine** (just north of town on Gold Hill) is now owned by the Julian Historical Society and is open for tours. Walking tours also are available at the **Eagle and High Peak Mine** (C Street, overlooking downtown).

Freed slave Albert Robinson and his wife Margaret built a two-story frame hotel in 1897 that he named after himself. When he died in 1915, Margaret continued to operate Hotel Robinson by herself. She sold the property in 1921, and the new owner renamed it **Hotel Julian**. The restored hostelry (2032 Main St.; 760-765-0201) has sixteen rooms. Listed on the National Register of Historic Places, it is the oldest continuously operating hotel in Southern California.

Built in 1888 as a blacksmith shop, the stone building now housing the **Julian Pioneer Museum** (Fourteenth and Washington; 760-765-0227) later was home to a brewery. In 1899 a new owner went back to blacksmithing.

Lake Tahoe (Placer and El Dorado Counties)

Led by the famous scout Kit Carson, US Army captain John C. Fremont and his men were the first white explorers to behold the nation's largest and highest alpine lake. Fremont decided to call it Lake Bonpland, for French botanist Aimé Bonpland, but changed his mind and named it Mountain Lake. The spectacular water body later was named Lake Bigler, for California governor John Bigler. Finally, in 1945, the California legislature approved its present name, "Tahoe" being a corruption of the native Washoe people's word for "edge of the lake."

The lake remained wild and desolate until the discovery of the Comstock Lode in adjacent Nevada in the late 1850s. As mining boomed in the 1860s, an estimated 80 percent of the timber around the lake was cut for use as fuel or lumber. Even as the trees around it were being felled, journalist Samuel Clemens, soon to be much better known as Mark Twain, said of the lake: "I thought it must surely be the fairest picture the whole earth affords." Reforestation took several decades after the silver bonanza was finally played out. Early in the twentieth century, the area began to develop as a resort.

In South Lake Tahoe, the largest community along the lake, the **Lake Tahoe Historical Society Museum** (3058 Lake Tahoe Blvd.; 530-541-5458) interprets the area's rich natural and cultural history. At Tahoe City, the North Lake Tahoe Historical Society manages a complex of three museums at **William B. Layton Park** (130 W. Lake Blvd.; 530-583-1762). The first is the **Gatekeeper's Cabin**, a reconstruction of the early 1900s Lake Tahoe Dam gatekeeper's residence. The gatekeeper's job was to regulate the flow of water from the lake to downstream users. Adjacent to the cabin is the **Marion Steinbach Indian Basket Museum**, which features more than eight hundred baskets crafted by eighty-five different California and Western tribes. The final history-related attraction here is the **Robert Montgomery Watson Cabin**, built in 1909. Due to the periodic wildfires that claimed earlier structures around the lake, the two-story log cabin is the oldest surviving structure in the area.

LONE PINE (INYO COUNTY)

Settled in the 1860s during the silver boom in the Sierra Nevada high country, Lone Pine and Inyo County offer visitors two versions of Wild West history—the one that really happened, and Hollywood's take.

Named for a solitary pine that once stood at the mouth of the canyon that flanks the town, Lone Pine began as a supply point for assorted area mining camps that are now ghost towns. Once the boom went bust, Lone Pine survived as a ranching and farming community until California became home to the motion picture industry, and the area's spectacular, yet diverse, landscape began to attract movie producers.

The first film crew came to Lone Pine in 1920, shooting an oater (early slang for a western) released as *The Last Roundup*, and the area continues to serve as the setting for feature films, television shows, and commercials. *Westward Ho!*, John Wayne's first Republic Pictures film, was shot here in 1935, and he went on to star in eleven more movies filmed in the area. In addition to studio-built Old West sets, over the years producers have further entwined the real and fictional Wests by shooting some films in actual old mining towns, including the Inyo County ghost towns of Cerro Gordo, Keeler, and Dolomite.

Overall, some four hundred western movies and one hundred television productions have been filmed in the nearby Alabama Hills, Owens River Valley, the Sierra Nevada, and Death Valley. The area's cinematic history is the focus of the 10,000-square-foot **Museum of Western Film History** (120 South Main St.; 760-376-4444). Opened in 2006 in an old Art Deco–style movie theater, this is the only museum in the United States dedicated solely to the western movie genre. In addition to its exhibits, the museum is home to a large archival collection documenting western film history. The museum also offers a brochure with directions to numerous movie landmarks in the area, including nearby Lone Ranger Canyon. Four miles from the museum, the canyon was the backdrop for the 1938 movie serial, *The Lone Ranger*.

The county seat of Inyo County is Independence, roughly sixteen miles northwest of Lone Pine. It is home to the **Eastern California Museum** (155 North Grant St.; 760-878-0258), which opened in 1928. The museum relates the history of Inyo County and the natural features and cultural aspects of the Eastern Sierra.

LOS ANGELES (LOS ANGELES COUNTY)

Most people see LA as La La Land, the City of Stars—not the forerunner of places like Virginia City, Deadwood, Dodge, or Tombstone. But some maintain that Los Angeles invented the Wild West. Not that anyone set out to develop a rowdy frontier culture; it just happened.

Founded by the Spanish in 1781, Los Angeles's Wild West heritage began with visits in the 1820s by some of the West's better-known figures, men like Kit Carson and Jedediah Smith. About the same time, an export market developed for cowhides, making Los Angeles the first cow town west of the Rockies. Then, five years before the discovery of gold in the foothills of the Sierra Nevada, a far lesser-known boom played out in Southern California. When the big gold rush began, ranchers from the Los Angeles area drove cattle to the mining camps, twenty years before Texas cattlemen started regularly pushing herds north to Kansas railheads.

In 1836, a dozen years before the Mother Lode gave birth to murder and mayhem in Northern California, Angelenos resorted for the first time to vigilantism to deal with a murderer. Many more lynchings would follow over the years. However, mob "justice" did not stop the killing. In 1850, Los Angeles experienced thirty-one homicides. By way of contrast, from 1870 to 1885, Kansas's five most famous cow towns (Abilene, Caldwell, Dodge City, Ellsworth, and Wichita) saw only forty-five killings combined.

When the well-known Wild West towns finally began to settle down, LA continued with its rough ways. In fact, in the nineteenth century more peace officers lost their lives in the line of duty in LA than in any other town. Stagecoach and train robberies in Southern California continued well into the 1890s.

As Los Angeles grew into a major metropolis, many of its early buildings, scenes of its misspent youth, were torn down. But many of its earliest buildings have been preserved within the city-operated **El Pueblo de Los Angeles Historic Monument** (bordered by Cesar Chavez Avenue, North Los Angeles, Alameda, Arcadia, and Spring Streets; 213-628-1274). Beyond El Pueblo, Los Angeles has more than 230 museums.

To get a feel for the LA area's Spanish colonial–Republic of Mexico heritage, visit **Mission San Gabriel Archangel** (254 South Santa Anita St., San Gabriel; 626-282-3181), **Mission San Fernando Rey de Espana** (15151 San Fernando Mission Blvd.; 818-361-0186), **El Molino Viejo** (1120 Old Mill Rd.; 626-449-5488), and **Los Encino State Historic Park** (16756 Moorpark St.; 818-784-4849).

Despite Los Angeles's relatively small Chinese population at the time, racial tensions between whites and Chinese had built to a dangerous level by the late 1860s. On October 24, 1871, rivalry between two Chinese factions led to a shooting. When two police officers arrived, one officer was wounded and a civilian who had accompanied them was killed. As soon as word spread that an Anglo had been killed by a Chinese man, a mob began to form. Soon, roughly five hundred men descended on Chinatown and a riot erupted.

By the next morning, eighteen Chinese men had been hanged in what stands as the nation's worst mass lynching. A Los Angeles County grand jury indicted twenty-five men in the deaths. Of those, ten stood trial and eight were convicted of manslaughter. But the convictions were overturned on a legal technicality, and the men were not retried.

No marker memorializes the massacre victims at the **Chinese American Museum** (425 North Los Angeles St.; 213-485-8567). Located in the 1890 Garnier Building, the 7,200-square-foot museum opened in 2003.

El Alisal

A man who would spend 143 days walking from Cincinnati to Los Angeles in 1884 to take a job might seem eccentric—especially when you consider that he built a house that looks like a small castle. He was a writer, which might explain it. Fortunately for posterity, one of the topics Charles Fletcher Lummis enjoyed writing about most was Southwestern history and American Indians. On his trek to California, for instance, he interviewed the outlaw Frank James. In New Mexico and Arizona, he filed dispatches on the ongoing Apache War. He went on to push for the preservation of California's missions and advocate for American Indian rights.

In 1895 he purchased a three-acre tract in Los Angeles and began building the house now known as **El Alisal** (200 E Avenue 43; 323-661-9465). Using smooth river rocks bonded with cement, it took him thirteen years to complete the 4,000-square-foot house where he'd live for the rest of his life. Today the house is owned by the City of Los Angeles and is operated as a museum.

In 1907, the writer founded the **Southwest Indian Museum** (234 Museum Dr.; 323-221-2164). The museum is now owned by the Autry Museum of the American West.

Wyatt Earp, with wife Josie, spent the last years of his life in a house in the West Adams neighborhood, one of at least nine rentals they are known to have had in the city. He died there on January 23, 1929, at the age of eighty. According to Josie, who was with him at the time, his last words, with nothing said before, were, "Suppose, suppose . . ."

The house no longer stands, but a historical plaque (4004 West Seventh St.) marks the site. The area isn't like it was in the 1920s. "Ironically, there is more risk of neighborhood gunplay today than when [Earp] resided there," a writer for the *Los Angeles Times* noted on April 1, 2011. The house where Josie lived after Earp's death still stands, at 1808 West 48th Street, Los Angeles.

The **Autry Museum of the American West** (4700 Western Heritage Way on the north side of Griffith Park; 323-667-2000) is not about the life of the singing cowboy from Texas, Gene Autry. While founded by the singer and film star, the museum's focus is the history and culture of the Old West. Its collection includes paintings by Frederic Remington, Charles M. Russell, and Edward Moran, as well as American Indian artifacts. Also displayed are guns, cowboy paraphernalia, and western movie memorabilia.

MARIPOSA (MARIPOSA COUNTY)

More than forty years before soldier, explorer, and future unsuccessful presidential candidate John C. Fremont founded Mariposa in 1849, a Mexican army officer saw swarms of butterflies along a creek in what would become Mariposa County. The lieutenant named the stream Las Mariposas, Spanish for "the butterflies." The colorful flying insects may have been plentiful in the area in 1806, but it was gold that later attracted placer miners and gave Mariposa the town its reason for being. It was the southernmost boomtown born of the Mother Lode. About the time the gold began to play out, Mariposa began benefiting economically from tourists coming to see what would become Yosemite National Park.

The Mariposa Historic District covers 1,200 acres and has sixty-one structures listed on the National Register of Historic Places. Many of the buildings date to the Gold Rush days, including the 1850 Fremont adobe, which served as Fremont's office. A self-guided walking tour of Mariposa historic sites is available through the Mariposa County Museum and History Center (see below).

The oldest courthouse in California—and for that matter, anywhere west of the Rockies—was built in 1854 from timber cut and milled nearby. Before other counties in this part of the state were organized, the two-story Greek Revival **Mariposa Courthouse** (508 Bullion St.; 209-966-2005) once served an area that covered about one-fifth of the state. Its courtroom, still in use, saw trials resulting from mining claim disputes to murder.

The **Mariposa County Museum and History Center** (10th and Bullion Streets; 209-966-2005) documents the history of the city and the county. It also features exhibits on some of the more notable trials that have taken place in the old courthouse over the years.

The **California State Mining and Mineral Museum** (5005 Fairgrounds Rd.; 209-742-7625) has more than 13,000 artifacts and mineral specimens related to the state's long mining history. Among the holdings is the Fricot Nugget, a 13.8-pound hunk of crystallized gold discovered in the American River in 1864.

Drinks Cost One Life and Twenty Years

As Lafayette "Punch" Choisser and a friend started to leave Joseph Biegler's saloon early one October morning in 1857, the German proprietor asked who planned to pay for their drinks. Choisser said he would, but wanted to run a tab. Biegler demurred. Words were exchanged, and Choisser pulled his pistol and hit the barkeep on the head with it. Despite the blow, Biegler went for his gun as Choisser headed for the door. Suddenly Choisser turned and pointed his pistol at the bar owner. At that, someone yelled for him not to shoot. He said he wouldn't, so long as Biegler put up his gun. When Biegler did that, Choisser rushed him, hit him again, and then shot him in the chest. "Punch" fled the bar but was later captured and tried in the Mariposa Courthouse. The judge sentenced him to twenty years in San Quentin.

MARYSVILLE (YUBA COUNTY)

Charles Covillaud, one of its founders, named Marysville for his wife, Mary Murphy Covillaud, a survivor of the Donner Party. The Feather River could be navigated as far as Marysville, so miners arriving by steamboat from San Francisco en route to the goldfields helped make it a lively place. Incorporated in 1850, by 1857 the town was one of the largest in the state.

For an overview of the town's history, visit the **Mary Aaron Memorial Museum** (704 D St.; 530-743-1004). A self-guided walking tour of historic downtown buildings, which includes nine listed on the National Register of Historic Places, is available there.

RIP, Black Bart?

The Wild West's most prolific stagecoach robber, Charles Boles—much better known as gentleman bandit Black Bart—disappeared after his release from San Quentin Prison and was never heard from again. According to Wiley Joiner's book, *Black Bart: The Search is Over* (Shalako Press, 2015), after leaving prison in 1888, Boles adopted a new alias—Charles E. Wells—and settled in Marysville. Joiner writes that "Wells" spent the rest of his life there as a law-abiding citizen, dying in 1914 at the age of eighty-four. While some disagree with Joiner's conclusion, the City of Marysville, which oversees the **Marysville Cemetery** (2063 State Highway 70; 530-749-3902), placed a gray granite marker at the outlaw's supposed grave that lists all of Boles's aliases.

The cemetery, believed to be the oldest city-operated cemetery west of the Mississippi, was established in 1850 and has some 10,000 graves. Due to vandalism, the cemetery is only open during the day and is locked at night. The supposed Black Bart grave lies on West Citizens Row, marker A743. The man who tracked Boles down, lawman turned private detective Harry Nicholson North (1835–1912), is buried in Oakland, California's, **Mountain View Cemetery** (5000 Piedmont Ave.; 510-658-2588).

Built in 1851 during the Gold Rush days, the **Silver Dollar Saloon** (330 First St.; 530-743-1558) dispensed drinks and for a time included a hotel. Black Bart, the stagecoach bandit, is said to have tipped a few back here. A brothel operated upstairs until 1972.

Monterey (Monterey County)

Settled by the Spanish in 1770, Monterey is California's second-oldest city. While much of its history predates or does not directly relate to the Wild West era, it is where the United States formally took possession of California in 1846, early in the Mexican-American War. Only two years later, with the discovery of gold in the foothills of the Sierra Nevada, the story of California and the West began a new chapter, epic in scope.

Remnants of Monterey's Spanish colonial and Mexican periods include the 1827 **Cooper-Molera Adobe** (506 Munras Ave.; 831-223-0172, ex. 776); the 1835 **Larkin House** (510 Calle Principal; 831-649-7188), and the 1843 **Casa Soberanes** (336 Pacific St.; 831-649-7118). "Path of History," a self-guided walking tour of these and more than fifty additional historic structures, including those that are part of **Monterey State Historic Park** (20 Customs House Plaza; 831-649-2907), is available through the park's visitor center.

The **Old Monterey Customs House**, built in 1814, is the oldest government building in California. During the time California was a Spanish colonial province and continuing after it became part of Mexico, the captain of any vessel wanting to trade at a California port had to register his ship's cargo in this building. Here on July 7, 1846, US Navy commodore John Drake Sloat raised the Stars and Stripes and declared California a US possession. The restored structure is part of Monterey State Historic Park. Built in 1854 with thick granite walls and used until 1956, the **Old Monterey Jail** (580 Pacific St.) never saw a successful escape.

Murphys (Calaveras County)

Once known as the "Queen of the Sierras," Murphys (no apostrophe) is one of California's better-preserved gold-mining towns. The first prospectors to find placer gold here were Canadian-born brothers John and Daniel Murphy, who in 1848 camped along nearby Angels Creek. Their camp became known as Murphys New Diggings, and later, Murphys Camp. While plenty of gold was being found in the area, the brothers decided an easier way to make money was to open a trading post. Doing business with American Indians and miners, they made their fortune, and departed in 1849. Their name stayed behind, though the town's name wasn't shortened to simply Murphys until 1935.

Before boom turned to bust, the area in and around Murphys produced an incredible amount of gold. Initially, a prospector could make a claim on an eight-foot-square area. One such claim was said to have netted its owner thirty-seven pounds of gold dust and nuggets in only one afternoon of panning. The next morning, that sixty-four-square-foot area yielded sixty-three additional pounds of gold. In all, an estimated $20 million in gold was extracted around Murphys before the supply diminished below the level of profitability.

While mining continued into the 1890s, production had peaked in 1855, the same year the two-story stone Sperry and Perry Hotel was built. It opened the following year and went on to accommodate numerous notables, ranging from Mark Twain before he became famous to business magnate J. P. Morgan, to another successful "businessman," stagecoach robber Charles E. Boles, much better known as Black Bart. The hotel's name was changed to **Murphys Hotel** (457 Main St.; 800-532-7684) after World War II, and it continues in operation today. Numerous other buildings from the boomtown days stand along Main, Church, Jones, and Scott Streets.

NEVADA CITY (NEVADA COUNTY)

Nevada City, known as the "Queen City of the Northern Mines," developed in 1849 about sixty miles north of Sacramento in a gorge formed by Deer Creek. Half the gold that came from the Mother Lode was mined in the vicinity. The town has more surviving Gold Rush–era structures than any town or ghost town in the California Gold Rush country. Fire ravaged most of the downtown area in November 1863, but the town quickly rebuilt, and many of those brick buildings still stand.

The Nevada City Chamber of Commerce (132 Main St.; 530-265-2692) has a self-guided tour of the old mining town's numerous historic buildings. The first stop is the chamber's building; the old office for the South Yuba Canal Co., dating from 1855, is the oldest building in town. In addition to the Firehouse No. 1 Museum (see below), the city has three other places to learn about its rich history: the **Nevada County Narrow Gauge Railroad and Transportation Museum** (5 Kidder Ct.; 530-470-0902); the **Doris Foley Historical Research Library** (211 North Pine St.; 530-265-4606); and the **Searls Historical Library** (161 Nevada City Highway; 530-265-5910).

While the town's firefighters were not able to save the business district in 1863, thereafter volunteers who kept their equipment in this building, and in nearby Firehouse No. 2, either did their job very well, or Nevada City was just lucky. Whichever, this 1861 building has a wide range of artifacts and exhibits, including a collection of Donner Party relics. Firehouse No. 2, also built in 1861, continues in use as a fire station. The **Firehouse No. 1 Museum** (214 Main St.; 530-265-5468) is maintained by the Nevada County Historical Society.

Construction of the **National Exchange Hotel** (211 Broad St.; 530-265-4551) began in 1854. The hotel opened in 1856, making it the oldest continuously operating hostelry in California, and one of the oldest west of the Mississippi. It has accommodated the infamous to the famous, ranging from the outlaw Black Bart to President Herbert Hoover. It changed hands in 2018 and underwent a $5 million renovation.

Built sometime before 1856, the two-story brick building known as **Ott's Assay Office** (130 Main St.) originally housed a drugstore. Next door stood a wood-frame structure that served as James J. Ott's assay office. It was in that building, destroyed by fire in 1863, that Ott tested what Nevada gold miners called blue mud, a type of clay they hated because it clogged their sluices. Still, the sample had been submitted to see if it had any gold content. Ott determined that the disparaged material was almost pure silver. His 1859 test results set off the Comstock Lode silver rush. When his office burned four years later, Ott moved into the adjacent former drugstore.

NEWHALL (LOS ANGELES COUNTY)

The historical significance of most cemeteries comes from their age and who's buried there. But Newhall, a community since absorbed into Santa Clarita, has a cemetery that was a historic spot before it came to be a graveyard.

During the Kern River gold rush in the early 1850s, a stagecoach stop first known as Hart's Station stood where the cemetery is today. Purchased in 1855 by Sanford and Cyrus Lyon, the combination inn and tavern took on their name. The stagecoaches that stopped at Lyon's Station originated in the then-small town of Los Angeles and continued to Sacramento and the San Francisco Bay area. In addition to accommodations for travelers, there was a store and post office, the nexus of what would become Newhall. Any trace of the stage stop is long gone, but a state historical marker telling its story stands at **Eternal Valley Memorial Park** (23387 Sierra Highway).

Melody Ranch

The Wild West still lived in the memory of many in 1915 when the first black-and-white, two-reel, silent western was filmed at the newly opened Monogram Studios in Santa Clarita Canyon. Now known as **Melody Ranch** (24715 Oak Creek Ave.; 661-259-9669), the property continues as a moviemaking venue.

By the time cowboy singer-actor Gene Autry bought the 110-acre ranch and its studio-constructed faux Western town in 1952, some 750 Westerns had been shot at this location. Under Autry's ownership, the ranch continued as one of the prime western movie locations. Most of the best-known western movie stars, including William S. Hart, Tom Mix, Gary Cooper, Roy Rogers, and John Wayne, figured in films made here.

The original set, an iconic false-front Western town recognizable to any vintage western movie buff, went up in flames during the devastating Placerita Canyon fire in the summer of 1962. Only the original plastered adobe entrance, an adobe house, an adobe village, and a few outlying frame structures survived the conflagration. However, more than the early-twentieth-century movie set was lost. Also destroyed was Autry's collection of old stagecoaches and early automobiles, the star's personal memorabilia, and an archive containing 17,000 recordings. Autry then sold off most of the ranch, keeping twelve acres as the retirement home of his horse Champion (the third of his movie steeds so named). When the animal died in 1990, Autry sold the property to Renaud and Andre Veluzat. The brothers rebuilt the famed Western town and constructed soundstages, and once again the ranch became a well-used location. The set includes seventy-four Old West–style false-fronts for exterior town shots and permanent interiors for everything from a jail to a church.

In 2001, the studio opened the **Melody Ranch Museum**, which showcases one of the planet's largest collections of movie memorabilia.

Another old Hollywood film star lived on a 166-acre ranch in Newhall in a 10,000-square-foot, twenty-two-room mansion. New York–born William S. Hart began his career as a stage actor, but in 1914, at age fifty, he switched to western movies. Soon, his realistic portrayal of Western characters shot him to stardom, putting him on the same level as Charlie Chaplin or Douglas Fairbanks. Starring in seventy silent feature films, Hart didn't have to worry about memorizing lines, but as the William S. Hart Ranch website notes, "his lifestyle was anything but quiet."

After retiring in 1925 to his **Horseshoe Ranch**, he built his Spanish Colonial Revival–style mansion, which even featured a bedroom for his dog. Living with his youngest sister, Hart occupied the house from 1927 to his death in 1946, at the age of eighty-one. In his will he left his property to Los Angeles County for use as a park and museum.

As he famously said late in life, "When I was making pictures, the people gave me their nickels, dimes, and quarters. When I am gone, I want them to have my home."

The **William S. Hart Regional Park** museum (24151 Newhall Ave.; 661-254-4584) preserves most of the items original to the house, from period furnishings to artwork (including works by Frederic Remington and Charles Russell) to Hart's wardrobe and memorabilia associated with his career. Some of the items on display at the museum physically link the western star to the real Old West, including a nineteenth-century fringed animal-hide vest decorated with red-dyed porcupine quills, presented to him by the Sioux people, and a white leather quirt given to him by his friend, Wyatt Earp. Elsewhere on the property, visitors can see a buffalo herd maintained there, a memorial to Hart's horse Fritz, and Hart's dog cemetery. The museum's archival holdings related to the actor are curated and held by the **Seaver Center for Western History at the Los Angeles Natural History Museum** (900 Exposition Blvd.; 213-763-3466).

OAKDALE (STANISLAUS COUNTY)

On the Stanislaus River near the Sierra Nevada foothills, Oakdale was founded in 1871 at the newly completed juncture of the Stockton and Visalia Railroad and the Copperopolis Railroad. Earlier, the future town site had been the location of a ferry crossing on the road from Stockton to Los Angeles. While often referred to as the "Gateway to Yosemite," the town bills itself as the Cowboy Capital of the World.

Unfortunately for Oakdale, two towns in Texas—Bandera and Stephenville—make the same claim. But whether they or Oakdale truly merit the title depends on the definition of "cowboy." Oakdale's argument would be stronger if it asserted itself as the "Rodeo cowboy capital." With more than forty professional rodeo world champions hailing from Oakdale, town promoters can make a strong argument to the title.

No matter whether Oakdale or one or the other of its Texas rivals are the true cowboy capital of the world, visitors to Oakdale can learn more about both kinds of cowboys—the ranch hands who make the cattle-raising business work, and the rodeo performers who win big belt buckles—at the **Cowboy Museum** (355 East F St.; 209-847-7049). Located in the former Southern Pacific Railroad depot, the museum covers all aspects of cowboying, from barbed wire and branding irons to fancy saddles and rodeo trophies.

OAKLAND (ALAMEDA COUNTY)

Oakland developed as a port city across the bay from San Francisco. During the Gold Rush era it was a major supply point. Incorporated in 1852, it got its next economic windfall when it became the terminus of the transcontinental railroad. Following the devastating 1906 earthquake and fire that leveled much of San Francisco, the city experienced exponential growth for a time.

The visitor center (481 Water St.; 510-839-9000) has brochures on Oakland historic sites and other attractions. The **Oakland Museum of California** (1000 Oak St.; 510-318-8473) covers California history, California art, and California natural sciences. The museum's extensive collection includes an 1875-vintage photographic portrait of Oakland's founder, a man with quite a history.

The second act of legendary Texas Ranger Jack Hays's law and order career took place in and around San Francisco across the bay from Oakland. It was on the East Bay, however, that the former ranger and San Francisco County sheriff helped build a city. In fact, he founded Oakland. He also was a stockholder in the Oakland Light and Gas Company, the founder of the Oakland Union National Bank, and he oversaw extensive real estate holdings.

Indeed, Hays proved as shrewd a businessman as he had been an Indian fighter and Gold Rush–era sheriff. In 1852 he bought extensive acreage along Temescal Creek and built an imposing two-story frame house on the land. Hays called his estate Fernwood, and died in his stately residence on April 21, 1883, at the age of sixty-six. His wife Susan sold the property to William J. Dingee, founder of the Oakland Water Company. Dingee built an even more imposing mansion on the property (apparently razing the old Hays house). Dingee's house was destroyed by fire in 1899, and the property was sold for subdivision as a residential development. The area is today known as Jack Hays Canyon. The former ranger's estate was where Morgan Avenue (also known as Hays Canyon Road), State Highway 13, and Thornhill Drive, Oakland, converge in the upscale Montclair neighborhood.

Jack Hays's grave is enough to give any cemetery significance, but the former ranger's final resting place is itself historical. Founded by a group of East Bay old-timers in 1863, the 266-acre **Mountain View Cemetery** (5000 Piedmont Ave.; 510-658-2588) was designed by Frederick Law Olmsted, the famed landscape architect who laid out New York's Central Park. Hays lies in Plot 2, Lot 15. A bronze plaque was placed on the gray-granite crypt in which he and his wife are interred.

Not long after his death there was a short-lived movement to have his remains exhumed and shipped to Texas. The *San Antonio Express* thought Hays should be returned to the Alamo City for burial. Reading that, the editor of the *San Marcos Free Press*, published at the Hays County seat, suggested that the famed former ranger be buried in the county that had been named in his honor. Nothing came of either proposal.

Oakland Native Novelist

Novelist Jack London, an Oakland native who captured Alaska's gold rush days with his classic *Call of the Wild*, spent a lot of time in **John Heinold's First and Last Chance Saloon** (48 Webster St.; 510-839-6761). The saloon opened in 1883 and is still serving drinks. **Jack London Square** (472 Water St.) is a modern entertainment and dining district on the waterfront. In addition to the First and Last Chance Saloon, there's a restored cabin (56 Jack London Square) made with some of the material taken from the cabin London lived in while in Dawson City, Yukon Territory, during the Klondike Gold Rush (also known as the Yukon Gold Rush).

Fifty-four miles north of Oakland, at Glen Ellen, California, the **Jack London State Historic Park** (2400 London Ranch Rd.; 707-938-5216) preserves the ruins of the two-story stone house in which London died in 1916.

OROVILLE (BUTTE COUNTY)

Oro is the Spanish word for gold, the discovery of that precious metal being the reason this Northern California town came to be. When a prospector named John Bidwell found gold nuggets along the middle fork of the Feather River on July 4, 1848, seekers of precious metal descended on the area by the thousands.

About ten miles southwest of the discovery site and the mining camp (Bidwell's Bar) that developed there, a supply center grew at the head of navigation on the Feather River. Someone thought to name the landing Ophir, a mining community and port in biblical times. The name held until 1854, when a post office was about to be established there. For whatever reason, Washington nixed the town name. That's when it occurred to someone that Oroville would be a fitting substitute.

Even after its wild and woolly gold boom days ended, the frontier mind-set lingered on in Oroville and surrounding Butte County. On July 19, 1881, a bully named Tom Noakes, a young man so mean he was known for slugging oxen in the head, hurled a rock that killed Andrew Jackson Crum, a well-respected pioneer. Noakes was jailed in Chico, about twenty-three miles northwest of Oroville. Realizing that Crum had a lot of friends angered by his senseless killing, Chico officers moved Noakes to the county jail in Oroville, hoping to stave off mob action. But even though the two towns were nearly a full day's horseback ride apart, a delegation of outraged Chico citizens made the trip.

When one member of the party knocked on the door of the sheriff's office and jail that night, he told the jailer he was there to deliver a prisoner from another town in the county. The jailer fell for the ruse, and when he opened the door, in rushed Crum's pals. Easily overpowering the jailer, the men escorted Noakes from the jail and took him to a ranch Crum had once owned. There they hanged him from a tree that Crum had planted years before. If county law enforcement made any effort to identify the perpetrators, no one was ever prosecuted for hanging the killer. Andrew Jackson Crum (1830–1881) is buried in the **Chico Cemetery** (881 Mangrove Ave.; 530-345-7243).

The **Butte County Pioneer Museum** (2332 Montgomery St.; 530-538-2542) is housed in a replica of a miner's cabin, built in 1932. As with many other mining boomtowns, Oroville had a large population of Chinese workers and their families. A red-brick structure built in 1863 as a Chinese folk religion and community center, now known as the **Chinese Temple** (1500 Broderick St.; 530-538-2496), has been owned by the City of Oroville since 1937. Listed on the National Register of Historic Places, the late Gold Rush–era building serves as a museum devoted to Chinese culture in the West.

PLACERVILLE (EL DORADO COUNTY)

On a cold January night in 1849, four men barged into a gambling establishment and relieved its two proprietors of $600. Foolishly, the robbers did not leave the booming mining camp known as Dry Diggings. The following day a group of miners seized the suspects and guarded them while other miners organized a jury and a panel of three judges, who convicted and sentenced them to thirty-nine lashes each. After the punishment was administered, the four men were told to leave Dry Diggings and not come back. The men doubtless would have been content to uphold their end of the bargain, but a few days later someone reported that three of the men had earlier murdered someone at another camp. Dry Diggings's unofficial law enforcers tracked down the raw-backed robbers and returned with the three accused killers. This time the self-appointed law enforcers didn't bother with the formalities of what came to be known as a miner's trial and promptly lynched the trio.

The three dead outlaws had the dubious distinction of being the first victims of mining camp vigilante justice in California. The summary execution also earned Dry Diggings a new name—Hangtown. That attention-getting name hung on until 1854, when townsfolk deemed Placerville a more respectable name for their community. The town grew both as a mining community and a supply center for area miners. When the boom subsided, Placerville managed to stay alive as the seat of El Dorado County.

The **El Dorado County Historical Museum** (100 Placerville Dr.; 530-621-5865) focuses on the history of Placerville (nee Hangtown) and the rest of the county, which includes the site of John Marshall's initial gold discovery and several other communities rich in Mother Lode history. The **Fountain-Tallman Museum** (524 Main St.; 530-626-0773), housed in a building dating back to 1852, tells the story of everyday life in Placerville during the boom times. A historical marker indicating the location of the triple hanging that earned Placerville its nickname is at 305 Main Street. The building that held the Pony Express office for Placerville in 1860–1861 still stands at Main and Sacramento Streets. **Gold Bug Park**, 0.9 mile north of US 50 on Bedford Avenue, was the location of 250-plus mines, including the Gold Bug Mine. Operated by the City of Placerville, the park includes lighted, stabilized mine shafts that can be toured and other gold-mining equipment and machinery.

Wheelbarrow Johnny

When a wagon train passed through South Bend, Indiana, in 1853, bound for the California goldfields, a young man named **John Mohler Studebaker** (called "J. M." by his family and friends) joined the group. J. M.'s older brothers had a wagon-making business, so he swapped a wagon they helped him build for his passage westward. Like almost everyone else on their way to California, even though he had learned blacksmithing and wagon-building from his brothers, J. M. wanted to prospect for gold. Arriving in Hangtown with just fifty cents to his name, he intended to leave for the goldfields as soon as he could raise a grubstake.

Meanwhile, a blacksmith had heard that the newcomer could work with metal and wood, and offered him a job. J. M. said no, but when someone who seemed trustworthy warned him that prospecting was a risky proposition, he decided to take the job. What his employer needed him to do was build wooden wheelbarrows, a piece of equipment in high demand.

Using his wagon-making skills, J. M. started making wheelbarrows that were quickly recognized for their quality. For the next five years, he built hundreds of wheelbarrows, earning him the nickname of "Wheelbarrow Johnny." But that wasn't all he earned. After five years, he had accumulated $8,000.

Returning to South Bend, John Studebaker bought into the family business. By 1868, he was president of the company, which had a nationwide reputation for building fine wagons. Studebaker continued as head of the company until 1917, long enough to see the family business transition from building wagons to manufacturing cars. The building that held the blacksmith shop still stands at 543 Main Street, Placerville. A historical marker summarizes the rags-to-riches Studebaker story.

RED BLUFF (TEHAMA COUNTY)

On the Sacramento River 115 miles northwest of Sacramento, Red Bluff was settled during the Northern California Gold Rush and quickly developed as a riverboat port and mining supply center. Originally called Leodocia, in the early 1850s it was renamed for the red-sand bluffs where it developed. River traffic dried up as irrigation lowered the depth of the river, but the town became a timber-harvesting, agricultural, and ranching center.

William B. Ide, president of the short-lived Bear Flag Republic in 1846, later lived in Red Bluff in an adobe house built in the 1850s. The restored structure is the centerpiece of **William B. Ide State Historic Park** (21659 Adobe Rd.; 530-529-5599).

In 1849, New Englander Sidney Allen Griggs contracted "gold fever" and headed west for California. Rather than undertaking an overland journey, Griggs sailed to Panama, traveled across the isthmus, and took another ship to San Francisco. For all that trouble he did not do particularly well at the gold diggings, so he transitioned to the cattle business in 1854. Later, he turned to raising sheep. In the early 1880s, having done much better as a rancher than a gold miner, he built a two-story Victorian house in Red Bluff. The house remained in the family until 1931, when it was purchased by the James Kelly family. In 1966 it was acquired by a nonprofit group, restored, and opened as the **Kelly-Griggs House Museum** (311 Washington St.; 530-527-1129).

The body of murdered Oregon cattle baron Pete French (see Burns, Oregon) was returned to Red Bluff for burial next to his parents in **Oak Hill Cemetery** (600 Cemetery Ln.).

Shasta State Historic Park (15312 State Highway 299 West, Old Shasta; 530-243-8194) preserves the ruins of the Gold Rush boomtown of Shasta City. Covering nineteen acres, the park is located thirty miles north of Red Bluff. Restored to its 1861 appearance, the old Shasta County Courthouse accommodates a museum focused on the history of this once-flourishing mining community.

SACRAMENTO (SACRAMENTO COUNTY)
Debt compounded by a bad marriage motivated John Augustus Sutter (1803–1880) to leave his native Germany in 1834 in search of a new start. He sailed for New York and on to California in 1839 by way of the Sandwich Islands (Hawaii). Granted nearly 50,000 acres by the Mexican government, he settled on the eastern bank of the Sacramento River near its confluence with the American River and established a combination fort and trading post that came to be called **Sutter's Fort**. By 1848 Sutter had built a small empire based on ranching and farming, but his fortunes would soon dwindle when

upriver from his trading post, one of his employees made a discovery that would alter California, and American, history—gold.

Sacramento is not only the capital of California, it's also the state's historical museum capital. The city has eighteen history-related museums, plus six more in nearby communities, though not all of them focus on Old West history.

Built on the highest point in the Sacramento River Valley, Sutter's Fort is where Sacramento—and the Euro-American settlement of California—began. The fort gave early settlers a place to buy or trade for much-needed and hard-to-come-by supplies, as well as a variety of services, including a blacksmith shop. Preserved as the focus of **Sutter's Fort State Historic Park** (2701 L St.; 916-445-4422), the site complements **Old Sacramento State Historic Park** (Second St. and Capitol Mall; 916-445-7387). Covering 296 acres downtown, the park includes fifty restored or reconstructed historic buildings, the largest cluster of ca. 1850–1870 buildings in California.

Long before anyone cared about gold, native peoples populated the future state. Opened in 1940, the **State Indian Museum** (2618 K St.; 916-324-0971) focuses on three major aspects of American Indian life—nature, spirit, and family. Cultural items on display range from a redwood dugout canoe to baskets and beadwork. One exhibit covers the life of Ishi, the last survivor of the Yahi Tribe, who died in 1911 after spending his last years relating his culture to anthropologists so that it would not be lost forever.

A larger-than-life bronze statue of a galloping horse and its Pony Express messenger marks the spot (Second and J Streets in Old Sacramento) where rider Sam Hamilton left at 2:45 a.m. on April 4, 1860, on the initial leg of the Pony Express's first West-to-East trip. As the inscription on the granite base of the 3,800-pound sculpture points out, the short-lived mail-carrying enterprise "ended California's isolation from the rest of the Union." Every aspect of artist Tom Holland's piece is faithful to the period, with one exception: Most of the time, contrary to popular belief, Pony Express riders wore skull caps, not wide-brimmed hats.

As a transportation, communication, and banking company, Wells Fargo was a significant part of westward expansion and development. The corporation operates two museums in Sacramento: one in Old Sacramento (1000 Second St., Old Sacramento; 916-440-4263), and the other downtown, at Wells Fargo Center (400 Capital Mall; 916-440-4161).

Businessmen Leland Stanford, Mark Hopkins, Charles Crocker, and Collis P. Huntington organized the Pacific Railroad Company in Sacramento on April 30, 1861. The Civil War had begun earlier that month, but those four men were looking past that. They would be building the western half of the first railroad that would connect the east and west coasts of a nation they were sure would continue to grow. (The three buildings that served as their headquarters stand in Old Sacramento at 220–226 K Street.)

The **California State Railroad Museum** (111 I St.; 916-445-7387) maintains sixty pieces of vintage rolling stock, including the CPRR locomotive *Jupiter*, the engine that pulled the first train eastward from California. Fewer than forty-five full-size steam locomotives manufactured prior to 1880 still exist in the United States, and this museum has eight of them. In addition to the restored locomotives and rail cars, the museum has permanent and rotating exhibits and an extensive archival collection. The crown jewel of the collection is a duplicate of the golden spike driven at the May 10, 1869, ceremony at Promontory Point, which marked the completion of the transcontinental railroad. The duplicate, previously unknown, was donated to the museum in 2005 by the heirs of David Hewes, who was from San Francisco and commissioned the gold spike used in the early-day media event. The public did not know that Hewes had a gold duplicate made until the family came forward. The original golden spike is exhibited at **Stanford University's Cantor Center for Visual Arts** (328 Lomita Dr., Stanford; 650-723-4177).

The **California Museum** (1020 O St.; 916-653-7524), originally known as the Golden State Museum, opened in 1998. This expansive museum tells the story of the nation's most populous state, with standing and short-term exhibits.

John Sutter Jr. (1826–1897), who became estranged from his famous father, John Augustus Sutter, and numerous other historical figures are buried in **City Cemetery** (1000 Broadway; 916-653-7524).

SAN ANDREAS (CALAVERAS COUNTY)

Named for the New Testament's Andrew the Apostle, San Andreas was first settled by gold miners in 1848. After the placer gold played out, the community continued to flourish as a hard-rock mining town. (Hard-rock mining is the extraction—often from underground tunnels—of ore containing minerals such as gold, silver, copper, and others.) Its post office opened in 1854, and in 1866, the town became the seat of Calaveras County. During the early boom days, the notorious outlaw Joaquin Murrieta sometimes hung out in the San Andreas area.

Built in 1867, the two-story brick **Old Calaveras County Court-house** served as county courthouse for ninety-nine years. In addition to other county offices, the building held a courtroom, sheriff's office, and jail. In 1893, the county's hall of records was erected in front of the older building. The two structures nearly touch and came to be looked on as essentially one building. In this building, on November 17, 1883, Charles Boles—aka, famed highwayman Black Bart—pled guilty to robbing the Sonora-to-Milton stage two weeks earlier. Superior Court judge C. V. Gottschalk accepted the plea and sentenced the gentlemanly outlaw to six years in San Quentin Prison. Added to the National Register of Historic Places in 1972, the complex now is home to the **Calaveras County Museum** (30 North Main St.; 209-754-4658).

SAN DIEGO (SAN DIEGO COUNTY)

San Diego's history goes back much further than the golden era of the Wild West. Founded as a Spanish mission and presidio in 1769, San Diego is California's oldest city. The coastal town grew slowly until 1885, when it gained a transcontinental rail connection. Within a decade the seaport's population had increased sevenfold, from 5,000 to 35,000.

There's a lot to see in San Diego, so it's best to start at the Visitor Information Center (996-B North Harbor Dr.; 619-737-2999) to pick up a guide to all the attractions. (As with most larger cities, there are a plenty of non-history-related things to see and do in addition to those included here.)

More than two centuries before Spain began colonizing Alta California, as they called it, in 1542 the explorer Juan Rodriguez Cabrillo found a large natural harbor that he called San Miguel. Anchoring his flagship, the *San Salvador*, he came ashore in one of the ship's boats, the first European to set foot on the West Coast. Standing on a hill overlooking downtown, a stone statue of Cabrillo commemorates the significance of his discovery. The large piece of public art is the centerpiece of **Cabrillo National Monument** (1800 Cabrillo Monument Dr.; 619-553-4285). Established in 1913, the 144-acre park has a visitor center that tells the story of Cabrillo's voyage.

The Spanish did not return to this area until 1769, when Father Junipero Serra founded the first of twenty-one missions that would stretch south to north from San Diego to Sonoma. The mission was moved to its present location in 1774. Five churches in succession have stood at the site. The one still in use today was built in 1931 as a replica of how the mission looked in 1813. **Mission San Diego de Alcala** (10818 San Diego Mission Rd.; 619-281-8449) has a museum devoted to its history.

San Diego began as a pueblo built around a rectangular plaza that dates to the early 1820s, when Mexico succeeded in its effort to violently separate itself from colonial Spain. The plaza, which came to be called Old Town, was the heart of San Diego for half a century before a more traditional downtown began to develop. In 1968, the six-block area came back to life as a state historic park. Five original adobe structures were restored, and additional period buildings were reconstructed. **Old Town San Diego State Historic Park** (4002 Wallace St.; 619-220-5422) has museums, retail businesses, and restaurants.

For more information on these venues, drop by the **Old Town San Diego Chamber of Commerce and Visitor Center** (2415 San Diego Ave., Ste. 104; 619-291-4903).

Albert Seeley ran stagecoaches between Old Town and Los Angeles, and in 1869 built a square, two-story barn for his horses and coaches. As his business grew along with the two cities the stage line served, Seeley built a one-story addition and assorted sheds. He also put up a windmill. The old barn was razed in the 1920s but rebuilt in 1974 by the state. Since then, instead of hay, horses, and stagecoaches, the stable houses a collection of nineteenth-century animal-powered vehicles, including a *carreta* (a cart drawn by oxen), a Concord stage, a huge freighter, and more. The **Seeley Stable** (2648 Calhoun St.; 619-220-5422) is part of Old Town San Diego State Historic Park.

One of the city's oldest neighborhoods, the **Gaslamp District** retains much of the nineteenth-century architecture that Wyatt Earp would have known when he lived here, including the 1874 Old City Hall, the 1888 Bank of Commerce, and the 1890 Keating Building. But when Earp walked the district's streets, this was where the city's saloons, gambling houses, and bordellos operated. Back then, and through the early twentieth century, the area was known as the Sting-aree neighborhood, because it was where all the rough characters hung out. The name eventually faded, but the area's seediness continued until it began to be redeveloped in the 1980s. Now many of the old vice dens have been restored to accommodate clubs, restaurants, and shops.

Formally known as the "Gaslamp Quarter," the sixteen-square-block rectangular area is bounded by Broadway and K Streets and Fourth and Sixth Streets. The nonprofit Gaslamp Quarter Historical Foundation offers a ninety-minute guided walking tour that leaves from the **Gaslamp Museum** (410 Island Ave.; 619-233-4692). The museum is in the 1850 Davis-Horton House.

Where Wyatt Earp Ate Oysters

He may have spent a fair number of years in high, dry desert country, but Wyatt Earp apparently liked his oysters. Earp and wife Josephine (often referred to as "Josie" or "Sadie") lived in San Diego from 1887 to the early 1890s. He operated four gambling halls in town, but the only building still standing where he spent time is the 1888 **Louis Bank of Commerce Building** (835 Fifth Ave.) in the city's Gaslamp District. An oyster bar was on the ground floor and Earp is said to have frequented the place. A brothel called the Golden Poppy operated upstairs. With elements of Victorian baroque revival architecture, the four-story building is leased as retail and office space.

Earp and Josie are said to have lived in **Horton Grand Hotel** (311 Island Ave.; 619-544-1886), then called the Grand Horton, for a time. The hotel was built in 1887 as the city was booming following the arrival of its first railroad two years earlier. The hotel faced demolition in the 1970s to make room for new construction. But rather than simply bulldoze the old hotel, workers took it down brick by brick, numbering each one so that it could be rebuilt at another location. That happened in 1986. Included in the new hotel was material from the old Hotel Brooklyn, which had stood adjacent to the Grand Horton and had been built about the same time.

SAN FRANCISCO (SAN FRANCISCO COUNTY)

San Francisco and the United States both got their start in 1776. But the thirteen British colonies that declared their independence from the Crown that year lay all the way across the North American continent from the natural harbor on the West Coast where Spain had just established Mission San Francisco de Asis (more commonly known as Mission Delores), and a presidio to protect it.

Built of adobe in 1776, the original mission is the city's oldest surviving structure. In 1791, a more substantial mission was completed at what is now 320 Delores Street. By the early nineteenth century, the mission had grown into a complex of buildings, from dormitories to a cloth-making facility. At its peak, **Mission Delores** had roughly a thousand native people who had converted to Christianity and a farming-ranching operation that tended to more than twenty thousand head of livestock. After the California missions were secularized, the mission continued as a church. Several different churches have stood at the site; the current basilica (3321 16th St.; 415-621-8203) was completed in the mid-1920s. It is open to prescheduled, docent-led tours. Adjacent to the church is the original Campo Santo, or cemetery. Dating to the last quarter of the eighteenth century and used until roughly midway into the nineteenth, it contains thousands of graves, both marked and unmarked.

When the United States acquired California from Mexico in 1846, San Francisco (first known as Yerba Buena) was still only a small seaport. But on May 12, 1848, a Mormon merchant named Sam Brannon rode into town from Sutter's Fort. Racing hell-for-leather down the street toward Portsmouth Square, he waved his hat in one hand and a bottle of gold dust in the other. "Gold! Gold! Gold from the American River!" he shouted.

Gold fever soon decimated the town's population, with just about every man who could do so heading for the diggings. Even the town's newspaper, *The Californian*, suspended publication. However, San Francisco did not remain a ghost town for long. Within two years, its population had swollen from fewer than a thousand to twenty-five thousand. Roughly a decade later, when the Comstock Lode was discovered in Nevada, in 1859, the city experienced a second boom. Completion of the transcontinental railroad in 1869 saw San Francisco become the largest city in the West, with 150,000 residents by 1870.

San Francisco abounds in historic sites, museums, and other attractions. Given all the choices, the best place to start your exploration is the downtown visitor center (749 Howard St.; 415-391-2000). Guidebooks and brochures are available, as well as several multimedia information sources. For years, the **Museum of the City of San**

Francisco had space in the 1915-vintage City Hall. The museum told the city's story through artifacts and photographs, but has since been reinvented as an online virtual museum (sfmuseum.org).

Presidio of San Francisco

Under three flags—Spain, Mexico, and the United States—the Presidio remained an active military post from 1776 to 1994. Built overlooking California's largest natural harbor, the presidio was intended to protect the province that Spain called Alta California from invasion by Russia or Britain, two other European powers then keenly interested in the Pacific West.

The original fortification was destroyed in an 1812 earthquake, but was rebuilt. After Mexico wrested control of Alta California from Spain in 1821, the presidio accommodated Mexican troops. Mexico, too, feared that another nation might try to acquire the Pacific coast. But by the mid-1840s, the threat to Mexican sovereignty was the expansion-minded US government, not any European power.

Indeed, in a war that started in the new state of Texas in 1846, the Republic of Mexico lost California, Arizona, and New Mexico to the then-seventy-year-old United States. For nearly the next half-century, troops stationed at the Presidio took part in the Indian Wars, as well as protecting San Francisco. Beginning with the Spanish-American War in 1898, the fort supported US military activities in the Pacific and, eventually, Asia.

Finally, in 1994, the US military determined that a presence in San Francisco was no longer critical, and abandoned the post. The 1,491-acre installation, which had grown into a large complex of seven hundred mostly historic buildings covering a park-like setting, overlooking the Golden Gate Bridge, was transferred to the National Park Service to become part of **Golden Gate National Recreation Area** (State Highway 1; 415-561-4700).

Organized in 1850, the **Society of California Pioneers** maintains a museum at the Presidio (101 Montgomery St., Ste. 150; 415-957-1849) and the **Seymour Pioneer Museum** (300 Fourth St.; 415-957-1849).

Portsmouth Square began as a potato field, but soon became the public plaza for Yerba Buena, forerunner of San Francisco. It was here in 1846 that marines under Captain John B. Montgomery first raised the US flag over San Francisco. The captain commanded the USS *Portsmouth*, which is how the square got its name. Two years later the square was where San Franciscans learned that gold had been discovered in the foothills of the Sierra Nevada. Five history-related monuments stand in or near the square, which is framed by Grant, Kearny, Washington, and Clay Streets.

The Madam of Waverly Place

Across Grant Street from Portsmouth Square is **Waverly Place**, the location of the city's first red-light district. The 1906 earthquake and fire did its own form of urban renewal, and the bordellos did not get rebuilt. But what did survive is the story of the district's most popular madam, Belle Cora, and her husband Charles. She ran a high-class place, the best in the city. Belle and Charles, a handsome Italian gambler, had worked their way through the mining camps before settling in San Francisco. All went well until a blue-nosed society woman tried to get Belle and Charles ejected from a theatrical performance. Belle refused to leave, so the woman and her husband stormed out.

A couple of days later Charles ran into the woman's husband. One thing led to another, and Charles shot and killed the man with his derringer. Belle hired the best lawyer in San Francisco to defend her husband, and he succeeded in getting the jury deadlocked. The state might or might not have retried him, but circumstances intervened. When Charles's friend James Casey killed a newspaper editor whose trial coverage he hadn't liked, the city's vigilance committee decided it would be in San Francisco's best interest to lynch Casey. And, for good measure, Charles Cora. After the May 22, 1856, double hanging, friends urged Belle to leave town, but she stayed on until her death a few years later.

In the **Mission Delores Cemetery** (3321 16th St.; 415-621-8203) Belle and Charles lie beneath a tall gravestone that features a bas-relief of a couple with their heads bowed. Belle joined her husband in death on February 18, 1862. She was only thirty-five. Casey and the journalist he killed, James King of William ("King of William" was James's unusual surname), are buried in the same cemetery.

The **Jackson Square Historic District** was the cheating heart of the Barbary Coast red-light district. (Of course, many customers—from Forty-Niners to sailors to traveling salesmen—were not married.) The area's pleasure palaces survived from the Gold Rush days to the early twentieth century. Not only that, most of the buildings they were in escaped destruction in the 1906 earthquake and fire. Today, though houses of ill repute are long gone, the area contains the oldest concentration of commercial buildings in the city.

The square is between Montgomery and Sansome Streets and the district lies between Broadway and Washington and Montgomery and Sansome. Fifty historic sites were designated by the city in 1996, each marked with bronze medallions and arrows set in the sidewalk along a 3.8-mile route called the Barbary Coast Trail. Jackson Square is on the trail, which stretches from the Old San Francisco Mint (5th and Mission Streets) to Fisherman's Wharf and Aquatic Park.

Pioneer Monument is itself a San Francisco pioneer. Originally sited just north of the city's main library, the monument was dedicated in November 1894. Clearly a sturdy piece of public art, the monument withstood the 1906 earthquake and fire that destroyed much of the city. Budgeted for $100,000 when that was a fortune, the monument features a large bronze statue of Minerva atop an imposing granite base, originally surrounded by five smaller bronze statues on their own pedestals. Each of these depicted various aspects of the state's history. To make room for a new library, in 1991 the monument was moved one block to the middle of Fulton Street, across a park from

City Hall, between the old and new libraries, at 147 Fulton Street. A plaque explaining the history of California Indians was placed near the monument in 1996.

One of the five sculptures encircling the larger bronze was *Early Days*, a work depicting an Indian kneeling before a robed priest and a California vaquero. This 2,000-pound bronze was removed on September 14, 2018, for what the city's art commission agreed was viewed by American Indians as an offensive reminder of their subjugation.

The Pants that Won the West

Many a Wild West character, from prospector to outlaw, died not only with his boots on, but in a pair of denim pants that came to be called Levi's. Manufactured by the San Francisco–based **Levi Strauss & Co.**, blue jeans became an American icon. Ubiquitous as Levi's were—and still are—the generally accepted history of these britches is as phony as the fake wear spots in the knees of some modern jean brands. The myth is that German-born Strauss arrived in San Francisco during the Gold Rush with a supply of canvas, intending to market tents to miners. Instead, he saw what they really needed were more durable pants and began making and selling dungarees cut from blue-dyed canvas. The truth is that Strauss ran a dry goods store and did not start making jeans until a tailor from Reno, Nevada, named Jacob Davis approached him about producing denim pants with pockets attached by copper rivets. They obtained a patent in 1873 for what they called "waist overalls," and the rest is fashion history.

Levis Strauss maintains an archive at its San Francisco headquarters (1155 Battery St.). The company's original records were destroyed in the 1906 fire, but the archive has all the records generated since then. Also, in a fireproof vault is the oldest-known surviving pair of jeans, made around 1890. They are valued at $125,000. From 1906 to 2011, the Levi's plant was at 250 Valencia Street. The building, now remodeled, still stands.

Wyatt Earp and wife Josie lived in San Francisco from 1891 to 1897, and spent some of that time in a house at 514-A Seventh Avenue in the city's Richmond District. This was in 1896, when that year's city directory listed Earp's occupation as "horseman." Earp did have an interest in the Ingleside Racetrack, but "gambler" would have been more accurate than "horseman." While the Earps were living here, William Randolph Hearst's *San Francisco Examiner* published a highly sensationalized, three-part account of Earp's life. The local notoriety this publicity earned him led to him being asked to referee the much-touted and soon highly controversial Bob Fitzsimmons–Tom Sharkey prizefight of December 2, 1896.

The former Earp residence, a Victorian duplex with an upstairs bay window for each apartment, is privately owned but visible from the street or sidewalk. Earp had a wooden horse stable behind the residence, a redwood structure that stood until it was razed around 1997 to make room for a carport. Later, in 1896, the Earps moved to 1004 Golden Gate Avenue, closer to the city's bars and gambling venues. Earlier, the Earps had lived at 145 Ellis Street (a seven-story building now occupies the location) and at 720 McAllister Street (a three-story apartment building is there today) with Josie's half-sister and her husband.

He Only Thought He Was Bulletproof

Little Pete, leader of the Sam Yup Tong—literally "hall" or "gathering place," *tong* came to mean a secret society, often criminal in nature—made big money running brothels, gambling houses, and opium dens. In building his empire, he was said to have killed two score or more men. Accordingly, the thirty-four-year-old Chinatown kingpin knew a man in his position couldn't be too careful. Wherever he went, a bodyguard and two German shepherds accompanied him. In addition, Little Pete (his real name was Fung Jing Toy) wore a thirty-two-pound chain-mail vest and a metal-lined hat. Finally, he always packed two revolvers. On January 23, 1897, Little Pete made the mistake of leaving his bodyguard behind and walked the short distance from his residence to the Wong Lung barbershop. As he sat in a chair, two men rushed inside and started shooting. Two shots missed, but two .45 slugs slammed into his head and he fell dead. No one was ever convicted of his murder, and the Chinese underworld passed into other hands.

Little Pete got his last shave at 817 Washington Street in Chinatown. The building was destroyed in the 1906 fire, and a gift shop now stands at the site. For an overview of the impact Chinese Americans have had on California and San Francisco history, visit the **Chinese Historical Society of America Museum** (965 Clay St.; 415-391-1188).

The **California Historical Society** (678 Million St.; 415-357-1848), founded in 1871, maintains a Mother Lode of historical material related to the state's history, including the Gold Rush era. In addition to its archival records, the society offers changing exhibits in its galleries. Located in a remodeled one-time hardware store, its galleries are closed between exhibits, but the research facility is open during regular business hours.

With all the gold coming out of the diggings in bottles and bags, a critical need arose for two things: a secure place to keep gold, and a safe way to transport it. That business need was met by two men whose surnames would become synonymous with the Wild West—Henry Wells and William G. Fargo. In March 1852, they organized Wells, Fargo and Company. The comma between their two names eventually went away, but not their San Francisco–based bank or the stagecoach operation they began. Soon, Concord stages rolled back and forth between the mining camps and boomtowns along the Mother Lode. Next came out-of-state stagecoach service to points east. Intrastate and interstate, a shotgun-armed guard rode each stage to protect its gold-filled strongbox. The **Wells Fargo Museum** (420

Montgomery St.; 415-396-2619) is located at the Wells Fargo corporate headquarters in the city's Financial District.

SAN JOSE (SANTA CLARA COUNTY)

A Spanish agricultural community established in 1777 as Pueblo de San Jose de Guadalupe, San Jose served as the first capital after the United States occupied California in 1846 during the Mexican-American War. Its streets were laid out in 1848, and two years later it became California's first incorporated city. By then, the city was prospering as a trade center for the goldfields of the Mother Lode. Its first railroad connection in 1864 furthered the city's growth. The downtown historic district has some 250 structures dating as far back as 1865.

San Jose's two oldest structures stand across from each other in the downtown area: the 1797 **Peralta Adobe** (175 West St. John St.), and the 1855 **Fallon House**, a Victorian residence built by Thomas Fallon, one of the city's earliest mayors. Both structures have been restored and are open to visitors. **History Park** (1650 Senter Rd.; 408-287-2290) is a collection of restored or reconstructed historic buildings. California's third-largest city and high-tech "hard drive" of Silicon Valley has other museums and attractions, but these are the only sites related to local history. Of interest in the New Almaden Valley, eleven miles south of San Jose, is the **New Almaden Quicksilver Mining Museum** (21350 New Almaden Rd. New Almaden; 408-323-1107).

Sarah's House

In 1862 Sarah Lockwood Pardee married an energetic, innovative New Haven, Connecticut, shirt maker named William W. Winchester. He could have done quite well in the clothing industry, but in 1866 he turned from garment making to gun manufacturing. By the early 1870s, the repeating rifle that bore his name had become a standard piece of equipment in the Wild West. Consequently, the weapon made the Winchesters exceedingly wealthy.

Winchester rifles killed untold numbers of people and animals, but when William died in March 1880, it was from tuberculosis. Six years after being widowed, Sarah left New Haven and headed west to San Jose. Having no shortage of funds, she purchased an eight-room farmhouse and began what has often been described as the world's longest home remodeling project.

Beginning in 1886, under her direction, the house grew from 8 to 160 rooms. Those rooms included 6 kitchens and 13 bathrooms. There are 10,000 windows, 2,000 doors, 52 skylights, 47 stairways, the same number of fireplaces, and 17 chimneys. The huge house covers 24,000 square feet. The estimated cost of the makeover would be more than $70 million in today's dollars.

The logical question is, Why did Mrs. Winchester do what she did? And therein lies the legend that gave the sprawling mansion—and top tourist attraction—its trademarked name, The **Winchester Mystery House** (525 South Winchester Blvd.; 408-247-2101). Given that Mrs. Winchester kept pretty much to herself, while spending an inordinate amount of money on her residence for no obvious reason, writers of sensational newspaper articles made up an explanation: Haunted by the spirits of all the people her late husband's product had killed, Mrs. Winchester believed she could only stay alive as long as she continued to work on her house. There are differing nuances, but the theme is the same. She was a rich, uber-eccentric widow who believed in ghosts.

The truth is much less interesting. All the stairways that go nowhere and doors that open into walls date back to damage done by the 1906 San Francisco earthquake. Mrs. Winchester did not rebuild the portions of the house that were destroyed; hence, the "mysterious" architecture. The spiritualism legend is simply an artifact of yellow journalism.

SAN LUIS OBISPO (SAN LUIS OBISPO COUNTY)

San Luis Obispo may be the only community in the West that arguably owes its existence to bears.

Spanish explorers in 1769 saw a lot of bears when trekking through a valley that extended to Morro Bay on the mid-California coast. Accordingly, someone in the expedition thought it fitting to call the area Canada de Los Osos, which translates to Canyon of the Bears. Three years later, recalling the abundance of bears in the valley, the commander of the Spanish presidio at Monterey dispatched a hunting party to the area in hopes of alleviating a severe food shortage. The bears were still in the area, but there were considerably fewer of them when the party returned to Monterey with twenty-five mule loads of dried bear meat.

The success of the hunt led Father Junipero Serra to establish a mission in the valley along San Luis Obispo Creek.

Founded in 1772, **Mission San Luis Obispo de Tolosa** (751 Palm St.; 805-781-8220) stands above San Luis Obispo Creek. It has exhibits detailing the multicultural history of the area, from the native Chumash people through the Spanish colonial period and the time of Mexican possession to the American settlement of California.

After California became a state, San Luis Obispo briefly acquired a nickname—Barrio del Tigre. In English, that's Town of the Tiger. But the only tigers prowling around did so on two legs.

The well-traveled road that had connected San Diego to Sonoma, the El Camino Real, made a convenient venue for highwaymen who sustained themselves by relieving travelers of their money.

When in the spring of 1858 a gang of eight outlaws perpetrated a robbery and kidnapping that left three people dead, a group of some of San Luis Obispo's most respected citizens decided they'd had enough. As had happened in Northern California during the Gold Rush, a vigilance committee was organized to deal with the crime problem.

Unfortunately for the bandits, they neglected to kill two witnesses. These survivors were able to identify the robbers, and the vigilantes took it from there, killing gang leader Pio Linares in a shoot-out and lynching six of his colleagues. The affair turned out to be California's deadliest lynching, although those who found themselves at the end of a rope didn't get to enjoy the honor. (The eighth member of the gang got the heck out of San Luis Obispo County while he was still in good health.)

Visitors can immerse themselves in the community's history at the **History Center of San Luis Obispo County** (696 Monterey St.; 805-543-0638). Housed in the 1905 vintage former Carnegie Library, the center features a museum and archival collection. The museum has produced a self-guided walking tour of sites associated with the city's vigilante days.

Sixty miles south of San Luis Obispo, **Mission de la Purisima Concepción de Maria Santisima**, established in 1787, is the best preserved of the twenty-one missions founded in California from 1769 to 1834. Restored by the Civilian Conservation Corps during the Great Depression, the old mission still has ten of its original structures, including living quarters, a blacksmith shop, and the church. In addition to interpretive exhibits at the visitor center, the park offers living history programs and docent presentations.

SAN SIMEON (SAN LUIS OBISPO COUNTY)

Located on San Simeon Bay about halfway between San Francisco and Los Angeles, the village of San Simeon began as a sub-mission of Mission San Miguel Arcángel, founded in 1797. During the period that California was part of Mexico, three large ranches operated in the area, Ranchos Piedra Blanca, Santa Rosa, and San Simeon. Following California's admission to the Union, the town of San Simeon developed as a whaling port. In 1865, wealthy western mine owner George Hearst purchased the 45,000-acre Piedra Blanca ranch and later expanded it to 270,000 acres. After whaling played out in the 1890s, San Simeon developed as a recreational destination.

The Chief

Like thousands of other early Californians, George Hearst arrived during the Gold Rush. He settled in San Francisco, where in the spring of 1863 his wife Phoebe gave birth to their only child, William Randolph Hearst. In 1887, then-senator George Hearst conveyed ownership of the *San Francisco Examiner* to his son, William. To sell papers, Hearst perfected the sensationalist style that came to be known as yellow journalism, and proceeded to build a newspaper empire. Hearst newspapers, particularly the *San Francisco Examiner* in the late 1890s and early twentieth century, helped transform Wyatt Earp from a gambler with a past into a famous character who would go on to become an American icon. Known to his employees as "the Chief," in 1919 Hearst began construction on a mansion at San Simeon overlooking the Pacific. Not completed until 1947, only four years before his death, it became known as the **Hearst Castle** (750 Hearst Castle Rd.; 800-444-4445). The 165-room mansion, a mixture of Spanish Colonial Revival and Mediterranean Revival architecture, is now a state historical monument. A visitor center features exhibits documenting the Hearst family history.

SANTA BARBARA (SANTA BARBARA COUNTY)

Lying between the Santa Ynez Mountains and the Pacific, Santa Barbara developed around a Spanish colonial presidio and mission.

The last of four military posts established along the Alta California coast, El Presidio de Santa Barbara was garrisoned in the spring of 1782, while on the other side of the continent the American Revolution was under way.

Along with similar fortifications in San Francisco, Monterey, and San Diego, the presidio played a key role during the time Spain held sway over California. The garrisons—each located on a natural harbor—protected missionaries and settlers, served as governmental hubs, and discouraged any other nation's thoughts of invasion.

With native Chumash people contracted as laborers, the Spanish military oversaw construction of a walled quadrangle consisting of whitewashed adobe bricks on a stone foundation. Local timber was used to support a red tile roof for soldiers' quarters, the commander's residence, and other buildings. While two artillery bastions on opposing corners made the presidio's purpose plain, the complex's most imposing feature was more pacific—the bell tower rising above a church.

In addition to the church at the presidio, in 1786, Father Fermín Francisco de Lasuén established **Mission Santa Barbara** (2201 Laguna St.; 805-682-4149), not far from the presidio. The old mission is the tenth of twenty-one missions built in California by the Franciscans, but it is the only one still overseen by the Franciscans. The present church building dates from 1820. The mission, which includes a historic cemetery, garden, and a museum, is open for self-guided tours.

Covering four blocks in downtown Santa Barbara, **El Presidio de Santa Barbara State Historic Park** (123 Canon Perdido; 805-965-0093) is operated by the Santa Barbara Trust for Historic Preservation through an operating agreement with California State Parks. A visitor center interprets the history of the presidio and the region's successive yet overlapping cultures.

The state has restored two of the presidio's original buildings and reconstructed others. One of the original structures, El Cuartel, served as a residence for soldiers and their families. It is the oldest structure in Santa Barbara and the second oldest in the state.

The park also features reconstructions of the **Buenaventura Pico Adobe**, a house built around 1830, less than a decade after Mexico won its independence from Spain. Exemplifying the architecture of the early statehood period is an adobe house built in 1856 by Jose Maria Rochin, whose wife was a descendant of the presidio's first comandante.

Elsewhere in the downtown area are four additional historic homes dating from 1817 to 1854. The **Santa Barbara Historical Museum** (136 East De la Guerra; 805-966-1691), operated by the

Santa Barbara Historical Society, documents the city's history and the cultures that contributed to it.

SANTA CLARA (SANTA CLARA COUNTY)

Santa Clara developed around Mission Santa Clara de Asis, founded in 1777 as the eighth of Alta California's twenty-one missions established prior to 1834. After the United States gained control of California in 1847, the community was incorporated in 1852.

Harry Love

Born in Vermont, Harry Love (1809–1868) survived his days as a sailor on the high seas, as a soldier in the Mexican-American War, as an Indian-fighting Texas Ranger, and, as leader of the California State Rangers, a gunfight with legendary Mexican bandit Joaquin Murrieta.

But getting along with a woman was another story.

After his three months of ranger service in California, Love used his share of the reward money he got for his role in killing Murrieta to buy a large tract of land in Santa Cruz County. In 1854, he married a widow named Mary McSwain Bennett. They had a stormy relationship punctuated by several separations and reconciliations. In 1866, she unsuccessfully sued for divorce. While Love may have taken that as a victory, a succession of misfortunes soon left him destitute. His wife evidently felt sorry for him and allowed him to live in a cabin she had built for him on her ranch, but not with her.

On June 29, 1868, Love was sitting on the front porch of Mary's house (where he was not allowed) when she and an employee showed up. Because Love refused to leave, Mary's employee, who may have been more than a hired hand, shot Love. It was only an arm wound, but infection set in and he died.

Love was buried in an unmarked grave in **Mission City Memorial Park** (420 North Winchester Blvd.; 408-615-3790), but in 2003 a grave marker summarizing his story was placed at the site.

SONOMA (SONOMA COUNTY)

In 1823, two years after Mexico wrested itself from Spain to become an independent republic, Father José Altimira established Mission San Francisco Solano in the Sonoma Valley. It was the only mission opened during Mexico's possession of Alta California, as the province was known, and the last of the twenty-one missions that spanned the future state in the eighteenth and nineteenth centuries.

Twelve years after the building of the mission, in 1835 the Mexican provincial government dispatched troops from the presidio at San Francisco to protect the province's northern frontier from American Indians inflamed over growing encroachment of their land. The possibility of encroachment of a different sort also was of concern to Mexico, given the presence of Russian traders on the upper California coast, only sixty-four miles to the north.

Soldiers under Mariano Guadalupe Vallejo—military commander and northern frontier colonization director—laid out an eight-acre central plaza and began building a two-story adobe fortification later known as the Sonoma Barracks. The military unit stationed at the post was disbanded in 1844, but the settlement that had developed around the now-secularized mission and the garrison continued. On June 10, 1846, a small group of American immigrants took over Sonoma in what came to be called the Bear Flag Revolt. They proclaimed an independent California Republic with Sonoma as capital, but it was short-lived. A month later, early in the 1846–1848 Mexican-American War, newly arrived US troops raised the American flag in Sonoma. California statehood, hastened by the discovery of gold in the Sacramento area, came in 1850.

The state acquired the old barracks in 1957, restored the building to its appearance at the time of the Bear Flag Revolt, and opened it as **Sonoma State Historic Park** (Spain St. at First St. East; 707-935-6832). In addition to the old military post, the park includes Mission San Francisco Solano, two historic hostelries—the Blue Wing Inn and the Toscano Hotel—and the former residence of military commander and town founder, Mariano Vallejo.

Fort Ross State Historic Park (19005 Coast Highway One; 707-847-3286) documents the history of a Russian colonial settlement established here on a mesa overlooking the Pacific in 1812. Built by the Russian-American Company, the fort served as an important outpost at the high point of Russia's colonial venture in North America. Chartered by imperial Russia, the fort was the southernmost settlement in that nation's North American land holdings, a vast area that included Alaska and part of California. Occupants of the fort grew crops to provide food for the nation's colder Alaskan settlements, traded with American Indians, and guarded against Spanish encroachment from the south. The outpost saw the construction of California's first windmills, and the first shipbuilding undertaken in the future state also occurred here.

The site was acquired by the state in 1906. The only remaining original structure is the **Rotchev House**. Alexander Rotchev was the last manager of Fort Ross. The fort's stockade, blockhouses, and other buildings, including a barracks, a powder magazine and fur warehouse, a Russian Orthodox chapel, another residence, and a windmill are all reconstructions based on archival research and archaeological investigations. Exhibits in the park's museum interpret the history of the site.

SONORA (TUOLUMNE COUNTY)

By the summer of 1848, it had become abundantly clear that the American River was not the only place gold could be found in the foothills of the Sierra Nevada Mountains. A party of miners from the Mexican state of Sonora began panning for gold in the area during the spring of 1849, which is how the mining camp that developed nearby came to be called Sonora. The community grew into the largest of the mother lodes, and the placer and hard-rock mining around it produced more than $40 million in gold. With more than fifty surviving structures from the Gold Rush era, Sonora—called the

Queen of the Southern Mines—is a bonanza for the history-minded. The town's Old West look has not been lost on Hollywood producers, who over the years have filmed scenes for numerous movies in the area.

Chilean miners discovered the deposit that became the **Big Bonanza Mine** in 1851. Initially it was a pocket mine, a pocket being a small, localized deposit of gold usually near the surface. In the 1870s a 1,500-foot shaft was sunk at the site so miners could start bringing up gold ore through hard-rock mining. In only one week in 1879, the Big Bonanza lived up to its name, producing 990 pounds of gold, worth $300,000 back then, and nearly $9 million in today's dollars. No accurate record exists detailing how much gold the mine produced during its life, but historians say it was in the millions of dollars. A historical plaque on a stone fence at North Washington and West School marks the site, which over time has been covered by pavement and houses.

In use since 1862, the **Old City Cemetery** (end of West Jackson St., Sonora) is the town's second cemetery, the only evidence of the first being a street named Cemetery Lane. The cemetery has 1,100 grave markers, even though at least 3,000 people were buried here. The graves represent a cross section of the former boomtown's history.

The **Tuolumne County Museum and History Center** (158 West Bradford St.; 209-532-1317) offers a self-guided tour of the town's historic buildings and sites. Founded by the local historical society in 1956, the center is in a building with its own history as the longtime county jail. Built in 1857 and rebuilt after a fire in 1865, the jail remained in use until 1951. Considering that the museum has an impressive collection of gold nuggets from the area, being in a secure building is an even better thing. In addition to exhibits on the county's history, gold mining in the area, and the California and Oregon Trails, the museum also holds an extensive collection of archival and genealogical material, including more than thirty thousand old photographs.

THOUSAND OAKS (VENTURA COUNTY)

Thousand Oaks was not incorporated until 1964, but its settlement dates to Spanish colonial times, when a large ranch was established in the Conejo Valley. Following California statehood in 1850, settlement began in this area in the mid-1870s.

The **Stagecoach Inn Museum** (51 South Ventu Park Rd., Newbury Park; 805-498-9441) is located in a reconstruction of the old Grand Union Hotel, a two-story frame hostelry built in 1874–1876 to accommodate stagecoach travelers. The original inn was given to the Conejo Valley Historical Society in 1964, then later moved to its current location and opened as a museum. A fire destroyed the historic building in 1970, but it was rebuilt and reopened as a museum. The museum covers the history of the Conejo Valley, from the American Indians who first lived here to the area's eighteenth-, nineteenth-, and early-twentieth-century history.

Wildwood Regional Park (928 West Avenida de los Arboles) covers 1,765 scenic acres in the western Simi Hills and Conejo Valley. Operated by the Conejo Open Space Conservation Agency, the park opened in 1967 and features twenty-seven miles of hiking trails. But long before people began coming to this area to enjoy nature, the landscape served as the backdrop for numerous western movies and television shows. Beginning in the early 1930s, when the property was part of the Janss Conejo Ranch, Hollywood producers influenced the way the world came to believe the Wild West looked.

Among the many movies that include exterior scenes shot here are three classics: *Davy Crockett, King of the Wild Frontier*; *The Man Who Shot Liberty Valance*; and *How the West Was Won*. Western TV shows with footage filmed here include *Bonanza*, *Wagon Train*, *Gunsmoke*, and *Tales of Wells Fargo*.

TRUCKEE (NEVADA COUNTY)

High in the Sierra Nevada, only a few miles east of the famous Donner Pass, Truckee was founded when the Central Pacific Railroad reached that point on April 3, 1868. Though the nearby Truckee River proved to be poor diggings for gold prospectors, Truckee flourished as a logging and milling center as well as a railroad town.

New life begins in the spring, and in April 1846 Illinois farmers George and Jacob Donner and their families joined a western-bound wagon train. Picking up the Oregon Trail in Independence, Missouri, the Donners and their fellow travelers reached a point in Wyoming where the wagon road forked. Rather than take the most-used route, the Donners decided to take a shortcut said to shave three hundred miles off the long journey. As it turned out, that was not a good decision.

After a grueling trek through the Utah desert, in late October the party reached a point near present-day Reno, Nevada. After resting a few days, the Donners and the other emigrants left in their wagons to traverse the Sierra Nevada in northeastern California. But heavy snow accumulations prevented them from going any farther, and they made camp for the winter just east of Truckee Lake, later renamed Donner Lake. Before spring came again, many of them died of exposure, starvation, and illness. At least two were murdered. After eating their livestock, most of those still alive resorted to cannibalism to survive. Of the ninety-one people who had been with the Donners when they left Illinois, only forty-five lived through that winter.

In 1901, the Native Sons of the Golden West began raising money to place a monument where the Donner Party had wintered. Set on a tall stone base, a bronze statue depicting a pioneer family was dedicated at the site on June 6, 1918. Three of the survivors attended the event. The state acquired the property in 1928 and developed it as the **Donner Memorial State Park**, later adding more acreage. Two miles west of Truckee, off I-80, the park's **Emigrant**

Trail Museum (12593 Donner Pass Rd.; 530-582-7894) has exhibits dealing with western expansion, the Donner Party, and the later history of the area.

Bad Blood Spilled Blood

Truckee's constable since 1869, fifty-seven-year-old Jacob "Jake" Tetter had a fine reputation as a lawman, and the record to back it up. In addition to ably handling all the routine duties a peace officer must perform, over the years Tetter distinguished himself by bringing in, alive, several noted bad men. For a time, he had a deputy named James Reed, who also proved to be an able officer.

But ill feeling developed between the two lawmen. Each saw the other as a political rival, and Tetter suspected Reed of involvement in a local vigilante group that had torched a Chinese workers' camp and opened fire on the men as they ran from the burning structure. One celestial had been killed. Though well-liked, Tetter drank too much and got crazy mean when he did. A feud with Reed that had been simmering for years finally boiled over on November 6, 1891, when the two ran into each other inside a saloon and had words. When Tetter went for his gun, Reed struck and disarmed him. Rather than go sober up, Tetter went home and came back with another handgun. He fired two shots at Reed and missed. Reed got off four shots at Tetter and did not miss. Mortally wounded, the veteran constable died at his residence the next day. A coroner's jury ruled that Reed had acted in self-defense.

The shooting took place in **Hurd's Saloon** (10072 Donner Pass Rd.), a brick structure built in 1870 that still stands. Tetter is buried in **Sierra Mountains Cemetery** (10370 East Jibboom St.; 530-587-6553). His grave lies next to that of his wife, who survived him by thirty years. Reed, the other combatant, died in 1905 of old age. He is buried in the same cemetery, though his grave is not marked.

Tetter was still constable in 1875, when for $1,235 (not counting iron work) the town's best stonemason built a sturdy new jail for the county. Its walls were thirty-two inches thick, and its ceiling was steel plate reinforced by narrow-gauge railroad rails. Each door to the lockup weighed about two hundred pounds. Constable Tetter booked the first prisoner on September 22, the same day the new jail was completed. The jail, with a second floor added in 1901, would last a long time, in use until 1964. Ten years later the Truckee Donner Historical Society began renovating the old hoosegow, which opened as the **Old Jail Museum** (10142 Jibboom St.; 530-582-0893) in 1976.

TULELAKE (SISKIYOU COUNTY)

Tulelake is a twentieth-century town, founded in 1937 near Tule Lake. Though only a small community, it is the nearest town to the scene of what some historians call the most vicious of all the western Indian conflicts—the Modoc War.

The Modoc had been relegated to a reservation in southern Oregon along with their longtime enemies, the Klamath. When the Modoc left the reservation in the winter of 1872 and returned to their homeland in the Lost River country of Northern California, the US Army set out to forcibly return them. The Indians fortified themselves in the rugged black lava beds near Tule Lake, and in the winter and spring of 1873 stood off hundreds of troops for six months. In the process, during peace negotiations under a flag of truce, the Modoc leader known as Captain Jack killed General Edward Canby and Reverend Eleazar Cady Thomas. (Canby was the only regular army general killed in any of the Indian Wars.) Six days later, troops again attacked the stronghold and found the Indians had left. The army pursued, and the Indians—initially only sixty warriors—eventually gave up. Captain Jack and three others were tried for Canby's murder and hanged, and others went to prison. The surviving Modoc were exiled to a reservation in Oklahoma.

Considering the ratio of deaths to the number of combatants, the war stands as one of the nation's costliest conflicts. Of six hundred US soldiers involved in the five-month war, fifty-three were killed—8.8 percent. In World War II, the combat death rate was 2.5 percent. Only fifteen Modoc died as a result of the war, just five in combat.

Much of the fighting occurred in what is now **Lava Beds National Monument**. The park is in a remote area of northern California. For directions, see nps.gov/labe. The visitor center (530-667-8113) has interpretive exhibits on the park's violent geologic past and its violent nineteenth-century history. Markers along self-guided trails interpret specific sites connected to the siege.

WEAVERVILLE (TRINITY COUNTY)

Named after John Weaver, one of the trio of men who raised the first cabin here, Weaverville was founded in 1850 during the Gold Rush. Many of its old buildings still stand, and someone who contributed greatly to Old West history but is virtually unremembered ended up buried here.

Dan Dedrick: Friend of Billy the Kid

After escaping jail in Arkansas, Dan Dedrick decided to go somewhere with more open country and less law enforcement. New Mexico Territory seemed a good choice. Arriving in 1877, he got involved in the Lincoln County War. Wounded in the five-day battle of July 1878, he had a bad arm for the rest of his life. After the shoot-out, Dedrick took up ranching, though his spread was more a safe place for cattle thieves than it was a more traditional enterprise. During this time, Dedrick became friends with Billy the Kid, which is how he ended up with a tintype of the only authenticated photograph of the outlaw. The famous image of the Kid standing with his 1873 model Winchester was taken in Fort Sumner in 1879 or 1880.

Not long after getting the picture, charges filed against Dedrick necessitated another cross-country move. This time he went to Northern California, got into mining, and did well. The community that grew up around his mine, long since a ghost town, was named Dedrick in his honor. In the early 1930s, Dedrick gave the tintype of Billy the Kid to his nephew. The nephew later gave the photograph to his sister-in-law, and she kept it in a cedar box for forty years, not realizing its significance. The Lincoln County Heritage Trust acquired it in the 1980s, but it was later returned to Dedrick's family. When the image went on the auction block in 2011, it brought $2.3 million.

Dan Dedrick (1847–1938) died in the small Trinity County town of Big Bar, and was buried in **Weaverville Cemetery** (100 Cemetery Dr., Weaverville; Row 43, Plot 21).

WHITTIER (LOS ANGELES COUNTY)

Whittier, named for the poet John Greenleaf Whittier, began as a Quaker community in 1887, though settlement in the area dates to California's day as a Mexican province. The town was incorporated in 1898 and grew as an agriculture center, becoming an important shipping point for produce following the arrival of the Southern Pacific and Santa Fe Railroads.

Pio de Jesus Pico (1801–1894) witnessed or took part in much of California's early history. After Mexico forcibly made itself independent from Spain, Pio Pico became governor of the Mexican province of Alta California in 1832, and was elected a second time in 1845. During the 1846–1848 Mexican-American War, he was a key figure in negotiating an early end to the fighting in California in 1847, which saved many lives and put California on the path toward statehood.

In 1848, Pico built an adobe house on his 9,000-acre ranch in what is now Whittier. The ranch house grew to a fifteen-room complex that since 1927 has been the centerpiece of **Pio Pico State Historic Park** (6003 Pioneer Blvd.; 562-695-1217).

WILLITS (MENDOCINO COUNTY)

First inhabited by the Pomo people, the Little Lake Valley was settled in the 1850s by ranchers and timber harvesters. Named for founder Hiram Willits, the town was incorporated in 1888. In the early twentieth century it prospered as a railroad stop.

One of the Wild West's lesser known but exceptionally sanguinary shoot-outs happened on the main street of Little Lake (later renamed Willits) in the middle of the afternoon on October 16, 1867. The deadly street brawl marked the bloody climax of a feud between the Frost and Coates families. Over the years, about as many theories on the cause of the feud have surfaced as the victims it claimed. The most likely issue seems to be lingering North–South animosities following the Civil War. The two factions got into a fight in front of Kirk Baechtel's (some accounts have it as Brier's) store and saloon on Election Day. Fisticuffs escalated to a knife fight, which led to shooting. When it was over, William Wesley Coates, Henry H. Coates, Joseph Albert Coates, Thomas J. Coates Jr., and Elisha Frost lay dead on the street. Abraham T. Coates died the next day. Two others suffered significant wounds but recovered.

Elisha Frost had five sons and a daughter. One of the boys, twenty-nine-year-old Elijah, joined his father in the cemetery after being lynched from a bridge north of town on September 4, 1879. Also invited to the impromptu necktie party were Abijah Gibson and Thomas McCracken. Their alleged crime? Stealing chickens and hams.

All the victims of the 1867 shooting are buried two miles southeast of Willits in **Little Lake Cemetery**, Section 1. Lynching victim Elijah Frost is also buried in Section 1, not far from his father. The **Mendocino County Museum** (400 East Commercial St.; 707-459-2736) focuses on the area's history.

Yosemite National Park

If any piece of land was worth fighting for, it was the Yosemite Valley, an area of scenic grandeur that for centuries had been the hunting and harvesting grounds of the Miwok people of the southern Sierra Nevada range. But when white settlers descended on California in the mid-nineteenth century, they were drawn to the Yosemite area in search of gold. Naturally alarmed at the intrusion, the Miwok violently resisted. That led to the 1851–1852 Mariposa War, during which the Miwok were driven out.

While some mining did occur in the area, gold prospectors did better elsewhere in Northern California. The real treasure of the Yosemite Valley, with its waterfalls, granite peaks, and giant sequoias, was in its beauty and restorative power. In 1864, even though preoccupied with trying to save the Union during the Civil War, President Abraham Lincoln signed the Yosemite Valley Grant Act, a Senate bill conveying the Yosemite Valley and Mariposa Big Tree Grove to California, "upon the express conditions that the premises shall be held for public use, resort, and recreation." Famed conservationist John Muir pushed to further protect the natural area, and in 1890 Congress designated it as a national park. Later, the state of California returned the land to the federal government. As had been the case with the earlier created Yellowstone National Park, the US Cavalry protected the 1,200-acre park prior to the founding of the National Park Service.

The **Yosemite Valley Visitor Center** (Yosemite Village; 209-372-0200) offers an overview of the park's natural history and the cultures that shaped its history. Visitors also can learn about the park's nonhistorical attractions. For the Old West history buff, the **Yosemite Museum** (Yosemite Village; 209-372-0200) houses more than five million artifacts and pages of archival documents relating to the multicultural history of the park. The museum has been a park fixture since 1926. The **Pioneer Yosemite History Center** (4100 Forest Dr., Wawona) is an open-air museum featuring a collection of old log buildings moved to the center from their original locations in the park. Among the structures is the former US Cavalry headquarters dating from the time the military supervised the park (1891–1914).

On its website, the National Park Service rightly calls Yosemite "a shrine to human foresight, the strength of granite, the power of glaciers, the persistence of life, and the tranquility of the High Sierra."

OREGON

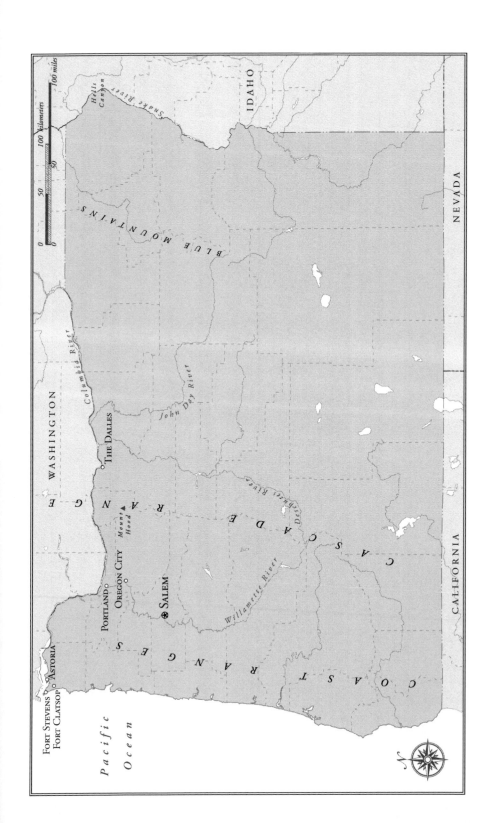

ALBANY (LINN COUNTY)

In 1847, brothers Walter and Thomas Monteith decided to cross the continent from their native New York to the Pacific Northwest. Connecting with the Oregon Trail in Missouri, they traveled the rest of the way in an ox-drawn wagon.

Though hundreds of thousands made the same trip, what the Monteiths did when they chose to settle on the east bank of the Willamette River—just downstream from its confluence with the Calapooia River—was a bit different. The brothers filed claims on adjoining pieces of land, each covering 160 acres. But rather than putting up two residences, they built just one using hand-hewn lumber that sat squarely on their joint property line. That got around the requirement that each claimant had to live on his property.

Soon the brothers acquired another 320 acres, setting aside 60 acres as a town site. They chose to name the new community after the capital of their home state rather than themselves. Meanwhile, they added on to their frame house in 1849 and completed it the following year. The finished two-story frame structure also accommodated the general store the Monteiths operated and for a time served as the new community's civic and social center. The house was remodeled in 1855 and 1880. Twenty-one years later, it was moved fifty feet from its original location. But despite its architectural evolution and slight change in siting, it has remained standing and is considered one of the most authentic pioneer residences in the Pacific Northwest.

After the first steamboat docked at Albany, Oregon, in 1852, the town grew as a trade center and the Monteiths prospered in business. The community's importance got another boost when it gained rail service in 1870, though that marked the beginning of the end of the town as a riverboat landing. With numerous Victorian-era houses and buildings, one hundred square blocks of the city are included in four National Register of Historic Places districts.

Operated by the Monteith Historical Society and owned by the City of Albany, the **Monteith House** (518 SW Second Ave.; 541-200-0421) has been restored to its mid-1850s appearance and its rooms filled with period furnishings.

The Drinkard Wagon

Eighteen miles southeast of Albany in Brownsville, the **Linn County Historical Museum** (101 Park Ave., Brownsville; 541-466-3390) tells the area's story from the time prior to the arrival of the first Euro-Americans to the present century. Housed in a former railroad depot built in 1909, the museum has on display one of the few surviving Oregon Trail wagons. The wagon brought William and Martha Ann Drinkard and their family to Oregon from Missouri in 1865, but the story behind their six-month journey was not typical.

William Drinkard, whose grandfather had fought in the American Revolution, enlisted in the Confederate army during the Civil War. Captured, he was sent to a prisoner-of-war camp in Iowa. There, he was offered release if he agreed not to bear arms against the Union.

Drinkard agreed to the terms of the parole, and his wife sold their house and most of their goods in Missouri and bought and outfitted a covered wagon. She loaded their five children and set out for Iowa to pick up her husband. Once William was free, the couple, along with several other family members, headed west along the Oregon Trail. Martha, pregnant with their sixth child, drove the wagon she had purchased while her husband handled the wagon carrying his mother and her possessions. Their children walked or rode horses.

The Drinkards got to Oregon in the fall of 1865. Early the following year, Martha gave birth to a daughter and went on to have six more children. She lived to the age of eighty-two, dying in 1918. Her husband had preceded her in death in 1887. They are buried in **Alford Cemetery** (Albany-Junction City Highway at Powerline Road, Harrisburg; GPS coordinates: N44° 18.60', W123° 07.72').

Astoria (Clatsop County)

Towering 125 feet above Coxcomb Hill, the observation deck atop the concrete-and-steel monument known as the Astoria Column offers visitors a sweeping view of this coastal city, while relating the history of Oregon and the Astoria region in a 525-foot mural that wraps around the column. Depicted by a series of twenty-six colorful friezes, the story told on the monument begins with the American Indians who had lived here for thousands of years, transitions to the Euro-American discovery of the Columbia River by merchant ship captain Robert Gray in 1792, and ends with the advent of Oregon's first rail connection in 1893.

In between, of course, was a great deal of other history, including the founding of Astoria as a fortified trading post in 1811. That came only six years after the famed Lewis and Clark Expedition finally reached the Pacific Ocean here at the mouth of the Columbia River. The oldest city in Oregon, Astoria also is the first American city established west of the Mississippi. Named for American Fur Company founder John Jacob Astor, the town developed as a seaport and commercial fishing center.

Built in 1926, the **Astoria Column** (1 Coxcomb Dr.; 503-325-2963) is the centerpiece of a thirty-acre park maintained by the nonprofit Friends of the Astoria Column. With artwork by Attilio Pusterla, the giant piece of public art was funded by the Great Northern Railway. Operated by the Clatsop County Historical Society in the 1904-vintage former Astoria city hall, the **Clatsop County Heritage Museum** (714 Exchange St.; 503-325-2203) has exhibits on the area's American Indians, immigrants, pioneers, local industries (in 1880, half of all the canneries on the Columbia River were in Astoria), and other aspects of the city's history. The museum also houses the society's research center and archival collection.

In 1805, the Lewis and Clark Expedition built **Fort Clatsop** as their winter haven, where Astoria would later develop. The fort consisted of several log structures protected by a fifty-foot-square log stockade.

While awaiting spring, the two captains in charge of the expedition worked on their journals and other notes, planned their return trip, and strived to maintain military discipline while the soldiers kept busy with various preparations that included everything from sewing elk-skin moccasins, one pair for each man, to molding bullets and smoking meat.

After the Corps of Discovery abandoned the fort in 1806, it quickly fell to ruin. In such a rainy, humid environment, the fort rotted away within a couple of decades. With a view toward its restoration, the Oregon Historical Society began trying to fix the exact site of the fort shortly after the turn of the twentieth century. But it was not until 1955—the one hundred fiftieth anniversary of the Corps' arrival here—that a replica of the fort was constructed. This structure stood until 2005, when it was destroyed by fire. In a way, this was a good thing, because archaeological work and careful study of early records resulted in a more historically accurate reconstruction that opened in 2006.

Fort Clatsop National Memorial (92343 Fort Clatsop Rd.; 503-861-2471) is part of the Lewis and Clark National Historic Park. A visitor center has interpretive exhibits.

A maritime "Boot Hill," the Columbia River Bar—where the Columbia meets the Pacific—is considered one of the most treacherous passages in the world. Some two thousand vessels, including more than two hundred large ships, have gone down at this point since 1792. The various disasters have claimed more than seven hundred lives. The story of this key western waterway is told at the **Columbia River Maritime Museum** (1792 Marine Dr.; 503-325-2323). Among the many artifacts on display at the museum are two guns from the USS *Sharp*, wrecked in 1846 when she ran aground on the bar. Beachcombers discovered the cannons in 2008.

For years, especially during the spring salmon run, Astoria was as wild and woolly as any booming Kansas cow town or California mining camp. In 1877 Astoria had forty or so saloons and no shortage of gambling joints and brothels. The area with the rougher places was known as Swilltown, as in where a thirsty commercial fisherman went to swill booze.

In one of the Old West's more unusual community cleanups, simple physics, not vigilantes motivated by misplaced moral righteousness, helped Astoria become more respectable. On July 2, 1883, a blaze that started at a sawmill spread along the wooden streets (built on pilings over water) that connected many of the town's buildings. As the fire spread, nervous saloon owners began rolling out their whiskey barrels, more worried about the product they dispensed than the buildings they sold it from. Rather than pitching in to help fight the growing conflagration, elements of the "rougher class" commandeered the booze and proceeded to get drunk as the fire still raged. Then they started looting.

The fire was finally brought under control, but not the boisterous boozers, who just for fun threatened to torch the rest of the town. A committee of concerned, sober businessmen worked with police and finally got the situation under control. That done, the group decided it was time to fish or cut bait regarding community standards. The committee decreed that henceforth, bars had to close at midnight. Two ex–city police officers who ran one of the town's saloons refused to do that and ended up barricading themselves inside their establishment, taking potshots at their former fellow officers. When the bar owners were ultimately arrested, the committee threatened to lynch them if they did not get out of town. Pleased with their progress, the committee told all Swilltown proprietors to vacate Astoria within twenty-four hours.

Just a Flip of a Switch

In 1894, Astoria resident Thaddeus S. Trullinger turned to new technology—electricity—to facilitate old technology: execution by hanging. Trullinger rigged the trapdoor of the Clatsop County gallows so that the sheriff could merely flip an electrical switch to release it. The device was effectively used only once in what turned out to be the last public hanging in the county. In time, legal executions in most states would be done by electrocution, considered a more humane method.

Trullinger (1867–1944) lies beneath a plain flat tombstone in **Ocean View Cemetery** (575 18th St., Warrenton; 503-325-7275). Trullinger's house (1445 Exchange St., Astoria) still stands.

No surprise due to its varied landscape, which ranges from rocky Pacific shorelines to snow-topped mountains to grassy plains, Oregon has attracted numerous film companies since the first movie was shot in the state in 1909. Several popular westerns, including *Paint Your Wagon*, *Rooster Cogburn*, *Maverick*, and *Indian Fight* were filmed in the state. Located in the old Clatsop County Jail, built in 1913 and used until 1976, the **Oregon Film Museum** (732 Duane St.; 503-325-2203) is devoted to this aspect of the state's cultural history.

BAKER CITY (BAKER COUNTY)

The Oregon Trail passed through the vicinity of what would become Baker City, but the town did not develop until the 1860s, when prospectors discovered gold in the area. It then became yet another Wild West boomtown. Thanks to the arrival of rail service and continued gold mining, by the beginning of the twentieth century Baker City was the largest town between Salt Lake City and Portland. For years, it was known as the "Queen City of the Mines." After gold production waned, the community continued to thrive as a timber, grain, and cattle center.

The 2,000-mile Oregon Trail ended near what became Baker City. Today it is home to the **National Historic Oregon Trail Interpretive Center** (22267 State Highway 86; 541-523-1843). The center's exhibits focus on the history of this key transportation route and the immigrants who traveled it. Some 300,000 people made it from the Missouri to the Columbia River during the height of the trail's usage from 1841 to 1861.

Housed in a 1920-vintage natatorium (it used to hold an indoor swimming pool), the 33,000-square-foot **Baker Heritage Museum** (2480 Grove St.; 541-523-9308), formerly the Oregon Trail Regional Museum, displays and interprets the region's history. Exhibits deal with mining, ranching, Baker City history, Chinese culture, and more.

Built in 1889 at the peak of mining activity in the area, the three-story stone hostelry currently known as the **Geiser Grand Hotel**—originally named Hotel Warshauer—was only the third structure west of the Mississippi to feature an elevator. A clock tower beneath a peaked cupola rises four stories above the main entrance and an ornate stained-glass window hangs above the lobby. Beneath the hotel, for the benefit of gentlemen guests, a tunnel led to the town's busy red-light district. Closed in 1968, the venerable accommodation reopened in 1993 as the **Geiser Grand Hotel** (1996 Main St.; 541-523-1889), following extensive renovations.

BEND (DESCHUTES COUNTY)

An agricultural and timber-harvesting town founded in 1900, Bend lies between the Deschutes River and the Cascade Mountains. Settlement in the area began in 1877 when a land claim at a 90-degree bend in the river was filed for what the petitioner called the Farewell Bend Ranch. When residents applied for a post office in 1886, the name of the community that had developed on the river was shortened to Bend.

Billing itself as the place where "The West Meets Wild," the non-profit **High Desert Museum** (59800 US 97; 541-382-4754) covers a 135-acre campus with a 28,000-square-foot museum and numerous outdoor features. The museum, a Smithsonian affiliate, focuses on all aspects of eastern Oregon's culture and landscape. The **Deschutes Historical Museum** (129 NW Idaho; 541-389-1813) concentrates on the history of Bend and Deschutes County.

BURNS (HARNEY COUNTY)

In the high desert country of southeastern Oregon, Burns began in the 1880s as a boisterous cow town, though the timber and milling industries eventually became its driving economic forces. Early settler and merchant George McCowan named the town for the Scottish poet, Robert Burns. Ranching had begun in the area in the 1860s, but cattle raising increased greatly following US Congress approval of the Desert Land of 1877. At one point, legendary cattleman John William "Pete" French (1849–1897) ran around 45,000 head of cattle on a dozen ranches covering 1.5 million acres.

The **Harney County Historical Museum** (18 West D St.; 541-573-5618) has several displays featuring items connected with Pete French. The **Harney County Library** (80 West D St.; 541-573-6670) has an extensive Western history collection.

Another Case of Self Defense

Ed Oliver had the means, motive, and opportunity to kill Pete French, and on December 26, 1897, that's what he did. The means was the six-shooter. His motive arose from a dispute between the two men over a road easement. French's property surrounded Oliver's smaller holding, and Oliver wanted a road in and out. Opportunity presented itself when Oliver confronted his adversary while crossing one of French's pastures. Oliver galloped his horse into French's horse, which led to French striking Oliver with his horsewhip, which led to Oliver shooting French in the head. Charged with murder, Oliver gained acquittal in arguing self-defense. Despite the favorable outcome from Oliver's perspective, many believed French's death involved a conspiracy. French's body was returned to California for burial (see Red Bluff, California).

Pete French's Round Barn

Most barns are rectangular, but cattle baron Pete French had a round horse-training barn built on his property in 1883. Listed on the National Register of Historic Places, the 100-foot-diameter structure is now an Oregon state historic park called the **Pete French Round Barn State Heritage Site** (52229 Lava Bed Rd., Diamond; 800-551-6949). Diamond is forty-three miles southeast of Burns.

ENTERPRISE (WALLOWA COUNTY)

Developers laid out a townsite with a view of northeastern Oregon's Wallowa Mountains in 1886, but staking out streets and lots proved to be an easier process than coming up with a name for the town. When people began buying lots in 1887, they considered a variety of names for the new community before finally settling on Enterprise. Whoever proposed the name argued that it reflected the enterprising nature of those who settled here.

Visitors approaching the **Wallowa County Courthouse** (101 South River St.; 541-426-4543) pass under a stone archway labeled "Wallowa County Pioneers." Two brass plaques on the 1936 monument list the names of 199 settlers who came to the county between 1871 and 1879, including the name of a mass murderer who never paid for his crime.

While unquestionably a pioneer, Bruce "Old Blue" Evans also led a notorious gang of horse thieves. In late May 1887, he and his gang were fleeing to Idaho with a remuda of stolen horses. Still on the Oregon side of the Snake River, riding on the bluff above Deep Creek, Evans and the others spotted a group of Chinese men below them panning for gold. Presented with such easy pickings, the gang decided to rob and kill the miners and opened fire on them with their rifles.

Leisurely picking targets, they shot them down, as one writer put it, like so many prairie dogs. By the time they ran out of ammunition, only one man remained standing, so the outlaws chased him down and beat him to death with a rock. Over the next several days, the gang went on to rob and kill other Chinese miners, the final death toll estimated at thirty-four victims.

The sheriff investigated the massacres, and when one of the suspected participants confessed and named the others in exchange for immunity, six of the outlaws were charged with murder. Of those, Evans and two others fled the state and were never found. The other trio went to trial, but their defense attorney convinced the jury that the killing had been done by the three missing men, and his clients were acquitted.

In 2012, another monument went up in Wallowa County, one dedicated to the memory of the slain Chinese and placed at the scene of the crime. A four-by-five-foot slab of gray granite, it is inscribed: "Chinese Massacre Cove—Site of the 1887 massacre of as many as 34 Chinese gold miners—No one was held accountable." The same verbiage is repeated in Chinese and Nez Perce.

The twenty-first-century monument to the victims of the massacre is in the **Hells Canyon National Recreation Area** in the **Wallowa-Whitman National Forest**, upstream from where the Imnaha River flows into the Snake River. Ranger stations can provide more specific directions to the site.

Opened in 1976 in the 1888-vintage former First Bank of Joseph—that town's oldest building—the **Wallowa County Museum** (110 South Main St.; 541-432-6095) holds a collection of artifacts and scrapbooks put together by the county's first historian, early-day county tax assessor John Harley Horner.

One of Oregon's most noted lawmen lies beneath a plain granite marker bearing only his name and the dates of his birth and death. Born to pioneer stock in Brownsville, Oregon, in 1852, James M. Blakely became the best known of four brothers who for years wore either a badge or a judge's robe. Blakely took up ranching in the late 1870s near Prineville, but circumstances soon redirected his career (see Prineville, Oregon). Blakely served two terms as Crook County sheriff before moving to Wallowa County, where he also served two terms as sheriff. In the mid-1880s, "four of us boys were in public offices," Blakely recalled in 1939. "I was sheriff of Crook county, Joe was sheriff of Gilliam county, Billy was sheriff of Umatilla county . . . and George was Wasco county judge at The Dalles."

Jim Blakely died at the age of one hundred, in 1953. The longtime sheriff is buried in **Enterprise Cemetery** (305 NE Alder St.).

EUGENE (LANE COUNTY)

In 1846, Eugene Skinner brought 1,200 colonists to the Willamette River. Friendly American Indians said he should build on high ground to stay safe from floods, and he took their advice. He put up a cabin that served as his residence and a trading post. Eight years later, he and a partner platted a town site. Rain easily transformed the new town into a sticky bog, which led to its unofficial name of Skinner's Mudhole. In 1853, Skinner moved the town to a better location, and it was named Eugene City. When the city was incorporated in 1862, "City" was dropped from its name. Eugene became an industrial and timber town, and later, the home of the University of Oregon.

The visitor center (754 Olive St.; 541-484-5307) can provide information on the city's historical sites and other attractions. Eugene has several museums, but the only one directly bearing on western expansion and Eugene's history is the **Lane County Historical Museum** (740 West 13th Ave.; 541-682-4242).

HAMMOND (CLATSOP COUNTY)

The army established **Fort Stevens** at the mouth of the Columbia River during the Civil War. Though updated over the years, the big guns at the coastal artillery post continued to be trained toward the Pacific until after World War II. The remnants of the fort are part of **Fort Stevens State Park** (100 Peter Iredale Rd.; 503-861-3170).

JACKSONVILLE (JACKSON COUNTY)

The discovery of gold in what came to be called Rich Gulch in 1851 led to the development of Jacksonville as a mining town. First called Table Rock City, it quickly grew into Oregon Territory's largest city. While that didn't last, even after the boom died down, the town hung on. Being bypassed by the railroad in 1884 did not help the already faltering economy, and Jacksonville lost the county seat to Medford in 1926. Slow to no growth for decades resulted in most of the town's older structures surviving into the modern era. Now a National Historic Landmark, Jacksonville has more than one hundred vintage structures and looks like a western movie set.

The **Southern Oregon Historical Society** maintained a museum in the 1883-vintage former Jackson County courthouse in Jacksonville until 2010, but closed it to concentrate more on programming. In nearby Medford, the county seat, the society has a research library (106 North Central Ave., Medford; 541-773-6536) open to the public.

JOHN DAY (GRANT COUNTY)

A lot of western towns were named for someone, from well-known local or national figures to land developers and railroad officials, but Oregon has a possibly unique exception: a community honoring someone's first and last name—John Day.

John Day the person was a Virginia-born, six-foot-two-inch hunter employed by John Jacob Astor's American Fur Company. But for somebody who became the namesake of two Oregon towns (John Day and Daysville), a major river, a fossil bed, and a dam, not a lot is known about him. What is known is that he traveled from St. Louis across the Rockies to the Northwest in 1811–1812. In the spring of 1812, he and another trapper were captured by a party of American Indians who relieved them of their furs and possessions and left them naked near the mouth of what was then called the Mau Mau River (soon renamed the John Day River). Day and the other man eventually made it to Oregon and told their story. Whether it was the grit that enabled him to survive or something else about him that stood out, it must have been notable. For a man who gained a measure of immortality as a place name, there are at least four different versions of how, where, and when he died. Where he was buried is another mystery.

"Golden Flower of Prosperity"

In 1887, Chinese immigrants Ing "Doc" Hay and Lung On entered into a partnership to establish a general store at John Day. They called their place Kam Wah Chung, which translates as "Golden Flower of Prosperity."

While Lung On made a success of the retail business, Hay gained a reputation as a healer who relied on herbal medicines. The two men lived in the building, which also served as a social center and place of worship for the local Chinese community. Before Hay died in 1952, he had a will prepared, donating the circa-1866 building to the City of John Day. The old building is now the **Kam Wah Chung State Heritage Site** (125 NW Canton St.; 541-575-2800). The interior of the store and apothecary shop looks much as it did in the 1940s, when a customer could still pay for a hit from a bottle containing rice wine and a pickled rattlesnake. Exhibits at the nearby visitor center relate the history of the establishment and the story of the men who ran it. Chinese culture in the West is also documented.

KLAMATH FALLS (KLAMATH COUNTY)

Founded in 1867, Klamath Falls developed as a timber industry and agricultural center. First named Linkville for the nearby Link River, the community grew along the Applegate Trail, a lesser-known spur of the famed Oregon Trail. In the early 1890s the town was renamed for the Klamath people, longtime adversaries of the Modoc people of southern Oregon and northeastern California. The "Falls" in the name refers to an unusual phenomenon first noted by the Klamath: When the wind blows strong from the south, it causes the Link River to flow upstream. That creates a cascading stretch of white water and small rapids suggestive of a waterfall. This still occurs.

When the US government consigned the Klamath and Modoc peoples to the same reservation, the Modoc went to war. The conflict led to the death of substantially more whites than American Indians. **Fort Klamath**, established in the area in 1863, played a strategic role in the 1872–1873 Modoc War. Four Modoc men were hanged at the fort that year for killing General Edward Canby, the highest-ranking US military casualty of the numerous conflicts with American Indians collectively known as the Indian Wars. The four condemned tribesmen were buried at the post.

The fort was abandoned in 1890. Eight acres of the former military reservation were later set aside as a park and home to the **Fort Klamath Museum** (51400 State Highway 62, Fort Klamath; 541-381-2230). Thirty-five miles north of Klamath Falls, the museum is housed in a replica of the original post guardhouse and stands at its original location.

Klamath Falls is home to one of the West's larger collections of American Indian artifacts, the **Favell Museum** (125 West Main St.; 541-882-9996). Founded by Gene and Winifred Favell in 1972, the museum holds more than 100,000 artifacts, including one of the rarest projectile points ever found in the West, a piece made from fire opal. A sheepherder discovered it in Nevada's Black Rock Desert in 1910. Now operated by a nonprofit organization, the museum also has a substantial collection of Western art, including Charles M. Russell's *The Scout*.

The history of Klamath County is the focus of the **Klamath County Museum** (1451 Main St.; 541-882-1000). Housed in a former National Guard armory built in 1932, the museum has artifacts, photos, and maps related to the Modoc War, as well as an archival collection, including a set of contemporary diaries with accounts of the war.

Also in Klamath Falls is the **Baldwin Hotel Museum** (31 Main St.; 541-882-1000). Located in the four-story former Baldwin Hotel that opened in 1908 and continued in operation until 1977, the museum chronicles the lifeways of earlier Klamath Falls residents, from a typical schoolroom to a photographic studio to a lawyer's office. One thing the four-story, artifact-full museum does not have is an elevator.

Oregon City (Clackamas County)

Oregon City became the territorial capital in 1848, the first incorporated city west of the Rockies. The town on the Willamette River developed at the end of the 2,000-mile Oregon Trail. Many of the city's historic structures still stand.

The **End of the Trail Interpretive and Visitor Information Center** (1726 Washington St.; 503-657-9336) is the place to start exploring Oregon City. The center is on land originally owned by George Abernethy, a merchant who became the first governor of Oregon Territory. He permitted new arrivals to camp and graze their livestock here before they moved on.

Operated by the Clackamas County Historical Society, the End of the Oregon Trail Museum opened in 1989. Later renamed the **Museum of the Oregon Territory** (211 Tumwater Dr.; 503-655-2866), it holds some thirty thousand artifacts, including a digitized photography collection of more than ten thousand images. The society also maintains the historic **Stevens-Crawford Heritage House** (603 Sixth St.), the museum's original home.

The Father of Oregon

Crossing the Rockies in 1824, **Dr. John McLoughlin** established Fort Vancouver in 1825, and four years later claimed land for Hudson's Bay Company, where Oregon City would eventually develop. In 1845, after buying back a portion of the land, the man known as the Father of Oregon built a house near the

Willamette Falls. The historic structure was moved to its present location (713 Center St.; 503-656-5146) in 1909 and became a unit of the **Fort Vancouver National Historic Site** in 2003.

PENDLETON (UMATILLA COUNTY)

The settlement that became Pendleton developed around a trading post opened in 1851, though it did not get a post office until 1865. First known as Marshall, the town was renamed to honor Ohio lawmaker George H. Pendleton, and incorporated in 1880. Sheep and cattle ranches were early key economic factors, and the cowboy culture has endured.

The **Tamástslikt Cultural Institute** (47106 Wildhorse Blvd.; 541-429-7700) tells the story of the Oregon Trail and the settlement of Oregon Territory from the American Indian perspective, and explores the culture of the Cayuse, Umatilla, and Walla Walla tribes. Operated by the Umatilla Valley Historical Society, the **Heritage Station Museum** (108 South Frazer Ave.; 541-276-0012) is housed in the town's former railroad depot, built in 1909, and focuses on Pendleton's history.

The Pendleton Round-Up

"This ain't my first rodeo" is a popular expression in the modern West, often invoked by someone wanting to assert the extent of their life experiences. Those five words also can be altered slightly to refer to someone else, as in, "This ain't his (or her) first rodeo."

While Texas claims to have staged the first rodeo (though a lot of folks in Arizona will argue that), and Wyoming has had an annual rodeo since before the Spanish-American War, Pendleton has been putting on a rodeo every year since 1910. The Pendleton Round-Up has grown ever larger and is a big deal on the rodeo circuit. Usually attracting some fifty thousand spectators, the Pendleton Round-Up is held every September. The **Pendleton Round-Up and Happy Canyon Hall of Fame** (1114 SW Court Ave.; 541-276-2553) has extensive displays on the history of the event.

Hamley and Company (541-278-1100), not counting a few years' hiatus, has been manufacturing saddles since 1883. Initially a harness and saddle-making shop, the company later focused solely on its saddles. Its craftsmen developed the "Association" style saddle that became a standard for professional saddle-bronc riders. The business closed in the late 1990s, but reopened in 2005 under new ownership. In addition to its saddles, the company sells general Western wear. Since 1905, the company has occupied a building at 30 Southeast Court, Pendleton.

PORTLAND (MULTNOMAH COUNTY)

A borrowed quarter and later a series of coin tosses shaped Portland's history. When William Overton and Asa Lovejoy stepped from their canoe onto the shores of the Willamette River in 1843, Overton thought the area a fine place to develop a town. With 25 cents loaned by Lovejoy, Overton filed a claim on 640 acres later platted for development. But he ended up selling his interest in the town site to one Francis Pettygrove. Originally from Maine, Pettygrove wanted to call the new town Portland. Lovejoy, from Massachusetts, liked the sound of Boston. Pettygrove won two out of three coin tosses, so Portland it was. Soon an anything-goes logging town and seaport, Portland's early years saw numerous saloons, opium dens, and gambling venues, along with a rowdy red-light district.

Shanghaiing Tunnels

When a tall-masted ship made port in Portland, crew members often decided the readily available pleasures ashore and the chance of striking it rich in the goldfields, or some other way, were far more attractive than life at sea, and jumped ship. Consequently, many captains of outbound vessels were willing to pay a finder's fee to any ruffian delivering a drunk or drugged man who could be pressed into service as a sailor. Called shanghaiing, the practice lasted into the early twentieth century. Something that has lasted even longer is the belief that a network of secret tunnels that facilitated shanghaiing and other nefarious enterprises exists beneath downtown Portland. But according to the Oregon Historical Society, while shanghaiing was real, the tunnels exist only in legend.

Respected Pioneer or Crooked Cop?

When **James Henry Lappeus** died, his obituary writer apparently opted not to speak ill of the dead. Instead, the newspaper piece cast Lappeus as an Oregon pioneer and respected former police chief—the city's first. "His administration was eminently satisfactory," the scribe wrote, "and he enjoyed the confidence of the people, and the respect and obedience of his subordinates."

Well, there was the time the chief arrested a man for blowing his son-in-law away with a shotgun. Not long after, in consideration of $1,000 subscribed by the defendant's friends and handed over by his wife, the lawman forgot to lock the man's cell door and he "escaped." Considerably better off financially, Lappeus eventually booked the accused killer again and later attended his hanging, Portland's first legal execution.

What both the obituary and the former chief's detractors did agree on was that for much of his law enforcement career, Lappeus owned the Oro Fina Saloon and a variety theater. Of course, the obituary overlooked the fact that the saloon also offered gambling, and that the "theater" provided interested customers a more intimate entertainment experience than a mere stage show.

Lappeus (1829–1894) is buried in Portland's **Greenwood Hills Cemetery** (9002 Southwest Boones Ferry Rd.) in Section 1, Lot 99, Grave 2. The **Portland Police Museum** (Portland Department of Justice Building, 1111 Southwest Second Ave.; 503-823-0019) tells the story of Portland's law enforcement history, from the nineteenth century to present day.

Still in use, the federal courthouse in downtown Portland, located on the eastern side of the square-block area known as Pioneer Courthouse Square, was first used in 1875, but it had been under construction off and on since 1869. Known as the **Pioneer Courthouse** (700 Southwest Sixth St.; 503-833-5300), it is the oldest federal courthouse in the Pacific Northwest, and the second-oldest federal courthouse west of the Mississippi.

The Gentleman Bandit

Ezra Allan Miner, better known as **Bill Miner**, started stealing horses and robbing stagecoaches as a teenager in California and Colorado. While no one disputed his criminal nature, by most accounts he was a nice-enough fellow, even polite. He came to be known as the Gentleman Bandit, but good manners or not, taking other people's horses and money was against the law, and he ended up in San Quentin Prison. Released in 1901, the fifty-five-year-old found that the Wild West he had known was fading. Trains had replaced stagecoaches for the most part, and people were excited about horseless carriages and the prospect of machines that could fly.

For a while, Miner tried his hand at making an honest living, but enjoyed no success. Seeing no practical alternative, Miner and selected associates took up train robbery. On September 23, 1903, he and several associates stopped the Great Northern

Railroad's Oregon and Washington Train No. 6 just east of Portland. Using dynamite, two members of the gang blew open the express car door expecting the occupants would emerge with their hands up. Instead, the railroad express messenger levered his Winchester and shot one of the robbers in the chest. The bullet kept traveling and wounded the train's engineer. Miner did not want to get anyone else killed, and ordered a retreat. But as the outlaws withdrew, the messenger wounded another of their number. Miner and the fourth outlaw split up, and Miner avoided arrest for the time being. However, he would be heard from again.

Frances Fuller Victor traveled to Oregon in 1864 with her second husband and settled in Portland. She started out writing poetry, graduated to dime-novel Western fiction, and by 1878, to scholarly historical writing. She did that while associated with historian Hubert Howe Bancroft, who produced a twenty-eight-volume *History of the Pacific West*. Her connection with Bancroft continued until 1890. But while Bancroft claimed to have written the entire series, later scholarship revealed that Frances is the one who actually wrote the histories of Oregon, Washington, Idaho, and other states. After retiring from the Bancroft project, she continued to write until 1900. She died in 1902 at the age of seventy-six.

Frances is buried in **River View Cemetery**, Section 15, Lot 4, Grave 3 (8421 Southwest Macadam Ave.; 503-246-6488). Not everyone gets a grave marker nicely summarizing their life, but thanks to the Daughters of the American Revolution, Frances Fuller Victor (1826–1902) is memorialized in stone as "Pioneer Writer and Historian."

Another famous Western figure buried in River View Cemetery is **Virgil Earp**, celebrated lawman and older brother of Wyatt Earp. Virgil was wounded in the October 28, 1881, O.K. Corral gunfight in Tombstone, Arizona, and again, this time more seriously, when an assassination attempt on December 28, 1881, left him with a crippled arm. Despite his disability, he went on to serve as city marshal in Colton, California, from 1887 to 1890. He died of pneumonia in Goldfield, Nevada, and his remains were taken to Oregon for burial in River View Cemetery. A low, polished cylindrical stone marks the grave (Lot 18, Section 15, Grave 1).

Begun at the turn of the twentieth century, the **Oregon Historical Society Museum** (1200 SW Park Ave.; 503-222-1741) tells the story of Oregon from its original American Indian inhabitants through the Lewis and Clark Expedition to Oregon's territorial days and then statehood. In addition to its 85,000-plus artifacts, the building houses the society's research library and photography collection.

PRINEVILLE (CROOK COUNTY)

A post office named Prine in honor of pioneer merchant Barney Prine was opened in 1871, but "ville" got tacked on the following year. Located on the Crooked River in what was then Wasco County, the city was incorporated in 1880 and enjoyed prosperity as a timber town and ranching center. When Crook County was created in 1884, Prineville became the county seat. Although the town did have a close call in 1911 when the railroad bypassed it, Prineville built its own connection to the mainline nineteen miles away and saved itself from becoming a ghost town.

The Vigilante War

During the California Gold Rush and continuing in some areas across the West into the 1860s, in the absence of a legitimate judicial system, vigilantes saw to the maintenance of law and order. But as more and more towns and counties became self-governing, the need for organized vigilantism faded. Lynching did not cease, but extralegal hangings tended to be spur-of-the-moment, not the work of an ongoing vigilance committee.

In Prineville, however, vigilantism broke out in the early 1880s. In March 1882, rancher Lucius Langdon murdered two settlers in a property line dispute. That sparked what former sheriff Jim Blakely later termed a period of "rule by gun and rope that is one of the blackest chapters in Oregon history." A vigilance committee lynched Langdon and one of his ranch hands and, operating under the guise of a stockmen's association, members proceeded to violently rid the county of other men they considered undesirable. During the day, they tended to their cattle businesses. At night, wearing masks, they took care of their "civic" duty as they saw fit.

At first the dark work was tolerated, but having gotten used to taking the law into their own hands, the night riders began to threaten or string up people simply because it suited their business interests. When a young jockey was found hanged, word spread that several of the vigilantes had done it because he had refused to throw a horse race they had bet on. Certain area residents who were not vigilantes were getting fed up with the violence.

Blakely organized an anti-vigilante group called the Citizens Protective Union. Others began calling them the Moonshiners—not because they ran illegal stills, but because they did their work, like the vigilantes, in the moonlight. Unmasked but armed, they patrolled the county at night to discourage the vigilantes.

Obviously, the vigilantes did not like what was going on and decided that Blakely would be the next person lynched. If anyone wanted to continue as a Moonshiner after that, the vigilantes would take care of them as well. The situation reached a crisis point when all seventy-five of the Moonshiners, each well-armed, surrounded a saloon where the vigilantes had gathered.

"If you think you can stop us, come on out and try it!" Blakely shouted to the men inside. Rifles raised, the Moonshiners stood silently, waiting for the vigilantes to come out. But they didn't. Humiliated, they never rode again.

The reign of terror over, Blakely took up more traditional law enforcement as Crook County's first sheriff in 1884.

Seventeen people connected in one way or another to the bloody 1882–1883 period of lawlessness and vigilantism in Crook County are buried in **Juniper Haven Cemetery** (1555 North Main St.).

Founded in 1969 and greatly expanded over the years, the **A. R. Bowman Museum** (246 North Main St.; 503-447-3715) includes the archives and library maintained in the Crook County History Center.

SAINT LOUIS (MARION COUNTY)

Founded in 1847 by a Jesuit missionary, Saint Louis is one of Oregon's oldest communities. By 1860 the small settlement that had grown around the Saint Louis Catholic Church had enough residents to merit establishment of a post office. The Post Office Department closed the facility in 1901, but the wooden church—built in 1880 after the original hewn-log sanctuary burned—continues in use. Nearby, the **Saint Louis Cemetery** is the final resting place of one of the West's pluckiest if little-known women.

Five years after the Lewis and Clark Expedition penetrated the Pacific Northwest, in 1810 an Iowa Indian named Marie Dorion and her two young children accompanied her husband Pierre Dorion on what became known as the Astor Expedition. Essentially following Lewis and Clark's route, the party made their way from St. Louis, Missouri, northwest to Oregon, where at the mouth of the Columbia River they helped establish a trading post for John Jacob Astor's Pacific Fur Company, essentially a subsidiary of Astor's American Fur Company (see Astoria, Oregon). In 1814, having moved to a trading post along the Snake River in what is now Idaho, Marie was informed by an American Indian scout that a party of Bannock warriors were stalking her husband and other trappers. With her youngsters in tow, Marie left to find her husband and warn him of the planned attack. But it was too late. When she reached where her husband and the others had been camped, she found Pierre and all but one of the trappers had been killed. And despite her care, that man soon died.

Gathering the horses that the Bannock had left behind, she rode back to the trading post. There she discovered that it, too, had been attacked and all its occupants slain. Alone in the wilderness with winter approaching, Marie survived for fifty days in the mountains, subsisting on horseflesh, trapped mice and squirrels, and frozen berries. When the spring thaw began, she made it to an American Indian village near what is now Walla Walla, Washington.

A respected figure in the Pacific Northwest, several sites along the Walla Walla River commemorate Marie Dorion as the Madonna of the old Oregon Trail. She died in 1850 at age sixty-four, having outlived two of her three husbands. She was buried at the **Saint Louis Catholic Church** (14084 Manning Rd. NE, Woodburn). Marie (ca. 1786–1850) was originally laid to rest beneath the altar in the sanctuary. When that church burned and was rebuilt, her burial site was forgotten. In 2014, the Daughters of the American Revolution placed a monument to her in the cemetery adjacent to the church.

SALEM (MARION COUNTY)

A few trappers and farmers lived in this area along the Willamette River beforehand, but the beginning of Salem traces back to the arrival of Methodist missionaries in 1834. The town was founded in 1842 and became capital of Oregon Territory in 1851. When Oregon gained statehood in 1859, Salem continued as the seat of government.

In 1866, the **Oregon State Penitentiary** (2605 State St.) was moved from Portland to Salem. Built of convict-manufactured brick and surrounded with fourteen-foot walls, the new facility looked as much like a fortress as a prison. The original prison stood well into the twentieth century before being replaced. The old lockup still stands, but since it's inside the twenty-five-foot walls of the still-in-use 194-acre prison campus, the only way to see the historic architecture up close is to commit a crime in Oregon or have a relative who did.

Wild Bunch gang member Harry Tracy and his brother-in-law David Merrill became inmates at the Oregon State Penitentiary on March 22, 1899. The twenty-four-year-old Tracy, a career criminal who had ridden with Butch Cassidy and the Sundance Kid had a penchant for jailbreaks, having already made escapes from prison in Utah (1897) and jail in Colorado (1898).

On June 9, 1902, armed with rifles that had been smuggled in, Tracy and Merrill shot their way out of prison in Salem, killing three guards and wounding one inmate in the process. For nearly two months, Tracy remained on the lam in Oregon and Washington State. During that time, he continued his killing. First, on June 28, he killed Merrill. Six days later, he killed two posse members and wounded a third. Two more officers died in another encounter he had with authorities that night. He made it to a farm near Davenport, Washington, where on August 5, he suffered a serious leg wound when cornered by five local citizens out to collect the reward that had been posted for the outlaw, dead or alive. Hidden in a barley field, he shot himself in the head with his .45 revolver. Not knowing for sure the nature of the final shot they heard, wary posse men waited until daylight before cautiously entering the field and finding their quarry dead.

The place where Tracy died became known as **Tracy Rock**, for a large geological feature nearby. It is on private property, the old Lou Eddy ranch, fifty miles west of Spokane near Creston, Washington.

Before Tracy's body was returned to Oregon for burial in the prison cemetery, acid was used to destroy his face to prevent anyone from trying to make off with the corpse to display the body for profit. His plain coffin filled with lime, he was buried in an unmarked grave. In 1931, Maurice Smith, who as a young attorney from Creston, Washington, had escorted Tracy's body back to Salem, visited the grave site. Later, the grave was covered with landfill, and finally, with concrete. The exact location is unknown today.

The Oregon Boot

In the early years of the Oregon State Prison, the facility had an embarrassingly high escape rate. That inspired Warden J. C. Gardner to come up with an innovative way of improving his retention statistics. He designed a device that could be attached to an inmate's leg that made walking difficult and running virtually impossible. The shackle—which the warden had inmates manufacture—consisted of an iron ring varying in weight up to twenty-eight pounds. Braces welded to the clamp-on weight connected to an inmate's footwear. Garden obtained a patent on the extremely painful, crippling device on July 3, 1866, and it was used routinely until 1878. When a new warden took over, Gardner got a court order barring the use of his invention unless he received a payment. After that, possibly into the late 1920s, it was used only for disciplinary purposes. **Oregon Correctional Enterprises** (3691 State St.) has one of the shackles on display.

The Marion County Historical Society Museum and Mission Hill Museum merged in 2010 to create the **Willamette Heritage Center** (1313 Mill St.; 503-585-7012). The center has acquired and restored fourteen historic buildings, some dating to the 1840s. Each of the structures has exhibits on some aspect of local and area history, including the Oregon Trail.

SEASIDE (CLATSOP COUNTY)

Most western towns developed as mining camps, cattle-shipping points, or railroad stops, but Seaside came to be as a resort in the 1870s. Ben Holliday, founder of the Overland Express, built a cottage there he called Seaside, and that's how the town got its name. In the 1880s and 1890s more lavish homes followed, and in 1899 the community was incorporated. Three Victorian-era houses are listed on the National Register of Historic Places.

The Sheriff and His Deputy Went Unarmed

When Clatsop County sheriff John W. (Jack) Williams and deputy Jim Lamar boarded the train for Seaside, they didn't think they'd need their guns. After all, they were investigating a burglary, not a major felony. When their train arrived from the county seat at Astoria, the two lawmen met with Seaside marshal A. E. Miller and Charles W. Fulton, owner of a summer home that had been broken into and then torched.

With a search warrant issued by the local justice of the peace, the three officers and Fulton went to a cottage occupied by Charles Willard. A mixed-race man who had ridden as an army scout during the Indian campaigns in Texas, Willard worked as a caretaker for several out-of-town summer cottage owners. After Fulton indicated that some of the things in the house were his, Williams told Willard he was under arrest. That precipitated a gunfight that left the sheriff dead and his deputy mortally wounded. Fulton pulled a concealed handgun and shot Willard twice. Marshal Miller, who had been wearing a .45, fired two more rounds and killed Willard.

Forty-four-year-old sheriff Jack Williams was the first Oregon sheriff killed in the line of duty. A Kentucky native, he is buried overlooking Young's Bay in Astoria's **Greenwood Cemetery** (91569 Highway 202). His gray granite tombstone is topped with an imposing stone statue of an Indian wearing a headdress and clutching a tomahawk.

THE DALLES (WASCO COUNTY)

The Dalles got its unusual name from French-Canadian explorers who used the French word for "slab" to describe a point where the Columbia River narrows into rapids over flat rocks. Lewis and Clark camped here in 1805, and Kit Carson passed through as scout for Captain John C. Fremont on the expedition's way to California in 1843. Until 1845, when a route was cut through the base of Mount Hood, The Dalles was as far as travelers on the Oregon Trail could go by land.

Established in 1850 as Fort Drum, the post was renamed **Fort Dalles** three years later. It served as a key installation during the Yakama War from 1855 to 1858. The military abandoned the garrison in 1867. The post surgeon's quarters, built in 1856, now accommodate the **Fort Dalles Museum** (500 West Fifteenth at Garrison St.; 541-296-4547).

The oldest courthouse west of the Rockies still stands, though not at its original location. Built in 1859, the two-story **Old Wasco County Courthouse** (410 West Second Place; 541-296-4798) included a jail, an office for the sheriff, and a courtroom. Wasco County was the largest county ever organized in the United States, once covering 130,000 square miles in what are now the states of Oregon, Idaho, Montana, and Wyoming. The building remained in use until a larger courthouse opened in 1883.

Pacific Northwest Cattle King

Ben Snipes came to the Pacific Northwest looking for gold, and found it—but the precious commodity that made him wealthy didn't come out of the ground. It ate grass and walked on four hooves.

Born in North Carolina in 1835, Snipes moved with his family to Iowa as a youngster. In the spring of 1852, at the age of seventeen, he joined a wagon train headed west on the Oregon Trail, paying for his passage as a livestock handler. Not long after the party reached the Salem, Oregon, area, Snipes took a job as a muleskinner on a pack train bound for the California goldfields. When they got there, Snipes bought pick, pan, and shovel, and staked a claim. Three days later he sold out for $500. The teenager then went to work for a butcher and soon ran his own shop, but the business failed when he extended too much credit.

When he heard of a major gold find on the Fraser River in British Columbia, Snipes bought a horse and rode north. He got there too late to stake a claim, but learning how scarce beef was, he realized good money could be made as a supplier. Back in Oregon, Snipes got a job as a drover on a herd to be marketed in the Cariboo mining district, an eight-hundred-mile journey. On his ride back to Oregon, seeing the rich grazing land in the Yakima Valley, he decided that the next time he pushed cattle to Canada, it would be his herd. Or, at least, partly his.

In the spring of 1856, he struck a fifty-fifty deal with a financial backer, hired some Chinook Indians as drovers, and made a second trip north. When the herd reached British Columbia, he sold the cattle at an astonishing $125 a head, for a gross profit of $12,750. After paying off his financial backer, Snipes went into the cattle business on his own, soon establishing a large ranch at the foot of what became known as Snipes Mountain, four miles west of Sunnyside, Washington. The cabin he built there in 1859 was the first non-Indian dwelling in the valley.

Despite heavy loss of livestock to severe winters, for a time Snipes ranked as the undisputed Cattle King of the Pacific Northwest. His kingdom collapsed with the coming of the railroad and cattle boats on the Columbia River, but by that time he had made enough to invest in other businesses. He bought real estate in Seattle, built a flour mill in The Dalles, and a three-story stone bank building in Ellensburg. The financial panic of 1893 bankrupted him, but he was working on building another fortune when he died in 1906. In 1958, Snipes was inducted into the National Cowboy Hall of Fame's Hall of Great Westerners.

Snipes is buried in the **Odd Fellows Cemetery** (900 West 18th St.). A one-and-a-half-story Colonial Revival–style house Snipes built in 1867 still stands at 218 W. Fourth St. in The Dalles, and is privately owned. The first cabin Snipes built on his ranch was later moved to Central Park in Sunnyside, Washington.

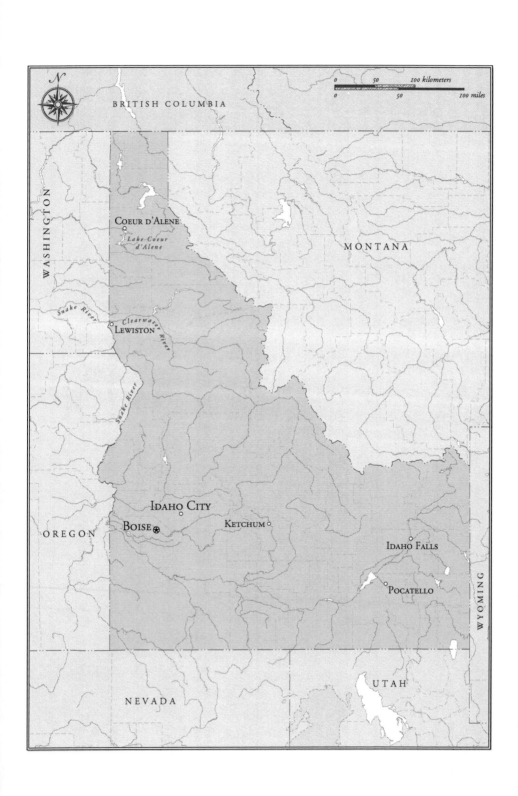

IDAHO

AMERICAN FALLS (POWER COUNTY)

People keeping written accounts of their westward trek on the Oregon Trail frequently noted that they could hear the tremendous waterfall on the Snake River well before they saw it. That fifty-foot waterfall gave this town a lasting name when it was founded in the early 1880s, but the waterfall disappeared under the waters of American Falls Reservoir with the damming of the river in 1927. Two years before the lake filled, the original town of American Falls was moved uphill to its present site, with the knowledge that the old location would soon be inundated.

Operated by the Power County Historical Society in a former hospital built in 1926, the **Power County Museum** (500 Pocatello Ave.; 208-226-1325) tells the story of the three American Falls entities—the drowned geologic feature, the old town, and the new town. Every summer, the releasing of water from the lake for irrigation reveals the foundations of the original community.

No massacre took place at what is now known as **Massacre Rocks State Park** (3592 North Park Ln.; 208-584-2672). However, just east of the present park, ten emigrants who had been following the Oregon Trail were killed in August 1862 when some two hundred Indians attacked their wagon train. Fighting continued for two days, with other travelers gathering at the geologic formation now known as Massacre Rocks for mutual protection. Some of the survivors may have scratched their names on a giant basalt boulder along the trail—a nineteenth-century graffiti site fittingly called Register Rock, now located about two miles from the visitor center. In addition to its recorded history, the park is interesting geologically, a boulder-strewn ancient volcano entered from the east by a narrow passage called Devil's Gate.

Ten miles west of American Falls, the visitor center has interpretive displays on the park's striking geological features, the Shoshone Indians, and the Oregon Trail.

BOISE (ADA COUNTY)

Even before the Oregon Trail was blazed, explorers and fur trappers working their way westward through the sagebrush-covered prairie delighted in the sudden appearance of distant cottonwoods, vegetation which meant shade and water. In 1832, when the swath of green came into view, someone among a party of approaching French-Canadian trappers shouted joyfully, "*Les bois! Les bois!*" ("The trees! The trees!") With an "e" added for good measure, the river along which the trees grew came to be called the Boise. A year later the British Hudson's Bay Company built a trading post at the mouth of the river, and in the early 1840s the Oregon Trail developed. Gold fever brought prospectors to the area, but the town of Boise did not develop until the US Army established a fort there in 1863 to protect the heavily trafficked emigrant trail. Three years later Boise became the capital of Idaho, but it remained a small town until it got a rail connection in 1887.

Fort Boise

Established in 1834 at the confluence of the Boise and Snake Rivers by Hudson's Bay Company, **Fort Boise** was an important supply point on the Oregon Trail. The trading post was abandoned in 1854 because of flooding and hostile American Indians. Learn about the fort at the **Old Fort Boise Replica and Museum** (305 North Third St., Parma; 208-722-5138), forty-two miles northwest of Boise.

Constructed in 1870 largely with convict labor, the **Old Idaho Territorial Penitentiary** (2445 Old Penitentiary Rd.; 208-334-2844) continued in use for 101 years—a period spanning Idaho's territorial days well into statehood. Apparently, no one considered the irony in laying the cornerstone on July 4 that year, given that independence was the last thing the lockup would represent. Beginning with one stone building surrounded by seventeen-foot-high walls, the prison expanded into a complex of structures, most dating to the nineteenth century. The prison had a section of solitary confinement cells known as Siberia and a room for gallows, used only once. Nine other men were hanged elsewhere on prison property.

Beginning in 1905, inmates were used to quarry and haul the sandstone blocks used in the construction of the **Idaho Capitol** (700 West Jefferson St.). Following major riots in 1971 and 1973, the prison was closed, and the inmates relocated to a new facility south of Boise. The old prison was reopened as a state-run museum, with a variety of exhibits on famous former inmates and prison life in general. It costs to see the museum, but unlike all the convicts the prison held over the decades, visitors are free to leave anytime they want.

With multimedia presentations and interactive displays, as well as more traditional exhibits, the **Idaho State Historical Museum** (610 North Julia Davis Dr.; 208-334-2120) explores the state's history and culture. Operated by the Idaho State Historical Society, the museum curates a wide range of artifacts, from clothing reflecting the heritage of the West to a replica of one of the 1,300-pound (empty weight) covered wagons that transported tens of thousands of immigrants to Oregon and California.

After the railroad reached Boise, the area's agricultural possibilities attracted a large influx of Basques. Soon, many of them took up sheep raising. The sheep market eventually declined, but Boise today has the largest Basque population outside Europe. The **Basque Museum and Cultural Center** (611 Grove St.; 208-343-2671) opened in the 1864 Jacobs/Uberuaga House (Boise's oldest structure) at 607 Grove Street in 1985, and expanded to include the adjacent building in 1993. The museum tells the story of the Basques in Boise and in all the West, where they were first drawn by the California Gold Rush. The museum and other historic buildings associated with the Basques make up the area of downtown that has become known as the Basque Block.

Idaho is nicknamed the Gem State for good reason: Two hundred and forty different minerals can be found within its boundaries.

Only two of those minerals, silver and gold, stimulated mining during Idaho's territorial days, but those precious metals, along with copper, zinc, and others, are still being produced. Housed on the first floor of the old dormitory for prison trustees, the **Idaho Museum of Mining and Geology** (2455 Old Penitentiary Rd.; 208-368-9876) opened in 1994.

CHALLIS (CUSTER COUNTY)

The quest for beaver pelts brought the first white people to the Salmon River country in 1822 when trappers with Hudson's Bay Company spent some time at the future location of Challis, and another party eight years later took thirty beaver and several buffalo in the area. But it was the prospect of finding gold that drew the first Americans to the Lost River Mountains. Their discovery of gold and silver in 1873 precipitated a boom that resulted in a scattering of remote mining camps like Bayhorse, Bonanza, Clayton, and Custer. Seeing a need for a better-located supply point, in 1876 Alvah P. Challis platted the town that would bear his name. When mining slowed down, the other places became ghost towns, but Challis lasted, even though it remained a small community. Surrounded by the largest wilderness area in the Lower 48, the 2.3 million–acre Frank Church–River of No Return Wilderness, the town has turned tourism into its new gold.

North Custer Museum (1205 South Main St.; 208-879-2846) interprets the area's history. A walking tour of the Old Challis Historic District, listed on the National Register of Historic Places, is available from the **Challis Area Chamber of Commerce** (700 Main St.; 208-897-2771). A historical marker on State Highway 75 near its intersection with US 93 explains a nearby bison jump site, where before 1840 Shoshone Indians harvested buffalo by chasing them to a steep precipice, forcing them to jump.

Custer and Bonanza, the larger of the old mining towns, are part of the **Land of the Yankee Fork State Park,** as is a giant twentieth-century mining artifact, the **Yankee Fork Dredge**. The General Custer, Lucky Boy, and Montana mines produced ample precious metal, but as the bonanza petered out, so did the towns. By 1911, they had been abandoned. Built in 1940, the 988-ton barge dredged gravel from the Yankee Fork until 1952. While the dredge recovered more than $1 million in gold and another $1 million in silver, it left behind five miles of tailings. Exhibits in the park's visitor center (24424 Highway 75; 208-879-5244) provide more details on the area's mining history.

A little over fourteen miles south of Challis is the ghost town of Bayhorse. Another Idaho mining boomtown, it dates from the 1870s, when silver was found in the area. The story is that the town was named for a prospector whose name no one seemed to remember. But folks did remember that he had two fine-looking bay horses, so to honor "that feller with the bay horses," the fast-growing mining camp became Bayhorse.

The town's peak years were in the 1880s, but the financial crisis of 1893, and the decline in the value of silver that soon followed, stunted the town considerably. Still, it kept its post office until 1927.

After everyone left, in time it became evident that it would be dangerous for anyone to go there. Toxic mine tailings, slag from smelters, and mining-related pollution (including arsenic) caused the US Forest Service—which owned the land—to declare the fairly well-preserved old town off limits. But in 2009 the federal government conveyed ownership of the site to the state, and the Idaho Department of Parks and Recreation undertook the task of cleaning up the town, eventually opening it to visitors. Directions to the remote site can be obtained at the Land of the Yankee Fork State Park visitor's center.

COEUR D'ALENE (KOOTENAI COUNTY)

Although the large natural lake fed by the Spokane River had been known to explorers and early French fur trappers, no settlement grew around it until after the army had established a fort on the edge of the lake in 1877–1878. The lake, the fort—and eventually, the town—were all named for the native Coeur d'Alene Indians. The military post later was renamed in honor of General William T. Sherman, who had selected the fort's site.

Fort Sherman was abandoned in 1900, and only three of its original buildings still stand—the post chapel, the powder magazine, and one of the officers' quarters. North Idaho College is on the land formally occupied by the fort.

Silver discoveries in the area gave the town its first economic boost, followed by logging, and later tourism. The **Coeur d'Alene Convention and Visitor Bureau** (105 North First St., Ste. 100; 877-782-9232) has brochures and tour guides devoted to attractions in the area.

Captain Mullan's Road

On the far side of the continent, his comrades in arms were fighting Southern secessionists at the beginning of the Civil War. But on July 4, 1861, Lieutenant John Mullan and his command had made camp in a mountain pass east of Coeur d'Alene Lake. The topographical engineer had earlier completed a 600-plus-mile journey on the road from Fort Walla Walla in Washington Territory to Fort Benton in Montana. Now he was headed west, making improvements to the road, which came to be called the Mullan Road. Much work remained to be done, but in observance of American independence, the troops fired their rifles and commemorated the occasion by carving "MR July 4, 1861" and their names into a large redwood.

Later known as Mullan's Tree, the redwood stood until it got hit by lightning. The portion of the tree bearing the old carving was removed to the Museum of North Idaho (see below). An interpretive marker explains the road construction project and the event that occurred at the site. Fifty-five miles southeast of Coeur d'Alene, the **Captain John Mullan Museum** (29 Earle St., Mullan; 208-744-1155) focuses on the story of Mullan and his road and the history of the old mining town that bears his name.

With permanent and rotating exhibits, the **Museum of North Idaho** (115 Northwest Blvd.; 208-664-3448) focuses on American Indians and all other aspects of the Coeur d'Alene area history. Opened in the old Fort Sherman powder magazine on the campus of North Idaho University in 1973, the museum moved to a larger, modern building in 1979.

GLENNS FERRY (ELMORE COUNTY)

Since its founding in 1869, Glenns Ferry has remained a small town, but at a nearby ford of the Snake River known as Three Island Crossing, travelers along the Oregon Trail faced one of the more momentous decisions of their lives. Not infrequently, if they made the wrong choice, it would be the last decision of their lives.

The question was whether to try crossing the river—very risky, if it had much flow—or take a longer, drier route. By 1869, the trail was little-used, so an entrepreneur named Gus Glenn built a ferry two miles upstream from the older crossing. The town that grew near the ferry took his name. (For whatever reason, the town is listed on the official Idaho state map without an apostrophe, which would correctly make "Glenn" possessive.)

Three Island Crossing State Park (1083 South Three Island Park Dr.; 208-366-2394) includes the site of the sometimes deadly crossing. The park's **Oregon Trail History and Education Center** has interpretive exhibits on the crossing and the dilemma emigrants faced. Wagon ruts left by the trail's 300,000 or more travelers are still visible in the 613-acre park. **Glenns Ferry Historical Museum** (161 West Cleveland Ave.; 208-366-2320) is housed in the old Glenns Ferry School, built in 1909 and used until 1965.

IDAHO CITY (BOISE COUNTY)

The discovery of gold in the Boise Basin in 1862 set off a rush that for a time ranked second only to the 1849–1850 California gold frenzy. At the height of the boom, prospectors averaged $220 a day in gold finds, and the area went on to produce some $250 million worth of precious metal. By 1863 Idaho City had become the newly created territory's largest city, with some fifty businesses—from respectable to disreputable—and a population exceeding six thousand. But only seven years later, in 1870, the area was considered "panned out," and Idaho City went into a slow but steady decline. Despite two devastating fires, many of its old buildings still stand.

One of those is the first territorial prison, built of hewn logs in 1864 at a cost of $10,975. The prison also served as the Boise County lockup, lodging many a miscreant miner among more serious criminals. It had to be moved from its first location to make room for a mining operation, and was relocated two more times before being moved to its present location in 1953, by the Sons and Daughters of Idaho Pioneers.

Operated by the Idaho City Historical Foundation, the **Boise Basin Museum** (503 Montgomery St.; 208-392-4550) occupies the former post office, a brick structure built in only twenty-nine days in 1867. Why the hurry? The previous post office had been lost in a fire that destroyed much of the town. Later it was used as a stagecoach stop, and later still, as a private residence. At the height of the mining boom, more than 1,700 Chinese workers and their families lived in Idaho City. From 1867 to 1885, a Chinese merchant named Pon Yam operated a store in a brick building at Montgomery and Commercial Streets. Today it houses the **Pon Yam Museum and Cultural Center**, also managed by the historical foundation.

IDAHO FALLS (BONNEVILLE COUNTY)

Once the sole province of the Shoshone-Bannock and Paiute people, the first settlement on the upper Snake River dates to 1863, when Harry Rickets established a ferry to accommodate travelers on the Montana Trail, the route gold seekers took from Salt Lake City, Utah, via Idaho to the newly discovered goldfields of western Montana.

As traffic on the trail increased, a man named Matt Taylor built a wooden bridge at a narrow point on the river about eight miles downstream from the ferry. First known as Eagle Rock, the crossroads town was renamed Idaho Falls in 1890, for the stretch of rapids at that point on the river. The community grew as a railroad division point and agricultural center.

The **Museum of Idaho** (200 North Eastern Ave.; 208-522-1400) interprets the history of the state, from the story of its American Indian peoples, the Lewis and Clark Expedition, the Oregon and California Trails, its mining history, and more. Operated by the Bonneville County Historical Society, the museum features standing and changing exhibits and has more than 25,000 artifacts in its collection. Opened in 1985 in the 1916-vintage former Carnegie Library, the museum has greatly expanded over the years, with two modern additions.

KELLOGG (SHOSHONE COUNTY)

This mining town, settled in the early 1890s, could have been called Jimmy, but then, who would want to name a town after a mule? Instead, folks thought it more proper to honor the mule's owner, one Noah Kellogg. He and his mule were held in local esteem because his long-eared critter supposedly kicked over a rock beneath which was found Idaho's richest silver vein. While likely mere legend, it is true that Kellogg was in the middle of Silver Valley and saw its glory days before the mines started shutting down.

The first settlement in the area came much earlier with the establishment of the Mission of the Sacred Heart by Father Anthony Ravalli in 1850. Hoping to convert members of the Coeur d'Alene people to Catholicism, the priest also converted some three hundred of the Indians into construction workers. The mission was built of straw, mud, and wood, the construction technique known as "wattle and daub." It took three years to build.

Ten miles west of Kellogg, **Old Mission State Park** (31732 South Mission Rd., Cataldo; 208-682-3814) preserves Idaho's oldest surviving building. An interpretive center features an award-winning, five-thousand-square-foot exhibit, "Sacred Encounters: Father De Smet and the Indians of the Rocky Mountain West."

The **Shoshone County Mining and Smelting Museum** (820 McKinley Ave., Shoshone; 208-786-4141) occupies the 1906 Bunker Hill Mine staff house, initially used as the residence of the general manager. When the mine closed in 1981, the structure stood vacant until it was conveyed for use as a museum. It opened in 1986.

KETCHUM (BLAINE COUNTY)

A silver and gold boom in the Warm Springs mining district necessitated a smelter, and after the facility began operation in 1880, a town grew around it. When a post office was applied for, Washington rejected the name the town had been using, which was Leadville. That's because Colorado already had a mining boomtown by that name. The federal turn-down led to the town being named for David Ketchum, a trapper who had earlier staked a claim in the area. After mining subsided in the 1890s, Ketchum became a shipping point for sheep raisers.

Twenty-mule-team wagons hauled more than borax in Death Valley. In the mining district around Ketchum, the giant wagons could carry up to twelve tons of ore per load. The **Ore Wagon Museum** (Fifth Street and East Avenue; 208-726-7820) displays a collection of the old wagons and the historical Bonning cabin. Twelve miles south of Ketchum in the county seat of Hailey, the **Blaine County Historical Museum** (1218 North Main St., Hailey; 208-788-1801) tells the story of Ketchum and Blaine County.

LEWISTON (NEZ PERCE COUNTY)

The discovery of gold in 1860 led to the founding of Lewiston at the confluence of the Snake and Clearwater Rivers, just east of the Oregon boundary. (At the time, however, what are now the states of Oregon and Idaho were part of Washington Territory.) Lewiston became the capital of newly created Idaho Territory in 1863, but that only lasted until 1864, when the territorial legislature voted to move the capital to Boise. The new town, and the gold camps around it, lay at the heart of the land long held by the Nez Perce, and that would lead to a tragic and bloody war.

As gold seekers and camp followers surged onto Nez Perce land, by treaty or presidential fiat, the federal government began acquiring the Nez Perce homelands. Many members of the tribe went along with the agreements, but a faction led by Chief Joseph, and later, his son, "Thunder Rolling in the Mountains" (also known as Chief Joseph), did not sign the treaties. In 1877, with the army authorized to use force if needed to move the so-called "non-treaty" Nez Perce to a reservation, Chief Joseph and his followers resisted. On June 17, a contingent of cavalry and volunteers clashed with the Indians in a battle that left thirty-three soldiers dead. After the engagement, known as the Battle of White Bird Canyon, Chief Joseph and about seven hundred of his people fled toward Canada through the Bitterroot Mountains and newly created Yellowstone National Park, and then across Montana. With the military pursuing relentlessly, a series of five battles followed before the Indians, only forty-one miles from the Canadian border, surrendered.

Congress approved creation of **Nez Perce National Historic Park** (39063 US 95, Lapwai, Idaho; 208-843-7009) in 1965, but construction of a park headquarters and museum did not begin until 1979. Opened in 1983, the park is made up of thirty-eight separate historic sites in four states associated with the Nez Perce War. Of those locations, twenty-six are in Idaho, on or near the Nez Perce Indian Reservation. The park headquarters is located ten miles east of Lewiston.

MONTPELIER (BEAR LAKE COUNTY)

A stopping place for travelers along the Oregon Trail first known as Clover Creek, Montpelier was settled by Mormons in 1864. Its name came from leader Brigham Young, who was born in Montpelier, Vermont.

The **National Oregon/California Trail Center** (320 North Fourth St.; 208-847-3800), considered one of the best of the various Oregon Trail museums, offers a tour conducted by living history docents that gives visitors a feel for what the six-month trek from Missouri to Oregon was like.

Lucky 13

On August 13, 1896, three men rode into Montpelier, hitched their horses outside the general store, and went inside. Finishing their business in the mercantile establishment, the trio untied their mounts and walked them down the street to the bank. There, one of the men waited outside with the horses while the other two entered the local financial institution.

Inside, they drew their pistols and ordered everyone to raise their hands, line up, and stand facing the wall. A short, stocky, blond-headed fellow, whose body language suggested he was the ringleader, watched the door while the taller man told the teller to hand over all the money. When the teller said he didn't have any money, the robber swung his six-shooter and refreshed the man's memory with a blow to the side of his head. Suddenly energized, the teller began stuffing cash into a bag the gunman handed him. The robber collected more money from the open vault and then grabbed a stack of coins behind the counter. Seeing a Winchester rifle hanging on the wall, the man took it as well.

While the blond covered those inside and told them not to leave for ten minutes, the tall man tied the money bag and rifle to his horse. Joined by the blond, the three men slowly rode out of town so as not to arouse suspicion. (Which calls into question the later claim by a former Bear Lake County sheriff's deputy that he had chased after the fleeing outlaws on his bicycle.) Out of sight at the edge of town, the robbers spurred their horses and galloped to a spot at Montpelier Pass, where they had fresh horses waiting.

With a take variously estimated between $5,000 and $16,500, Butch Cassidy (the short man), Ezra Lay (the tall man), and Wilbur Meeks (the outside man) galloped across the Wyoming line, only about fifteen miles from Montpelier. The posse that pursued them returned to Montpelier to report that the outlaws had disappeared.

The old bank still stands, now housing the **Butch Cassidy Museum** (833 Washington St.; 801-706-4004). The bank vault that held the money that the Wild Bunch gang "withdrew" from the bank is still in the building. One of the exhibits deals with the number thirteen, which kept showing up in Cassidy's life: He was born on April 13 as the oldest of thirteen children; he robbed the bank at 3:13 p.m. on August 13. Before doing so, the story goes, he deposited $13 so he could scope out the place.

MURRAY (SHOSHONE COUNTY)

Andrew Jackson Prichard was scouting the Coeur d'Alene River valley looking to lock in a good timber-harvesting deal when he found something that had to be dug up, not sawed down—gold. More than twenty years after Idaho's first gold boom, Prichard's discovery set off another stampede in 1883. Three mining camps developed in the area, but Murray was the only one to survive into the twenty-first century. During its glittering years, Murray attracted the usual human mining slag, saloon keepers, con artists, gamblers, and prostitutes.

Housed in a two-story, wood-frame, boom-era building, the **Sprag Pole Museum** (6353 Prichard Creek Rd.; 208-682-2009) began in 1933 when the new owner of the property found an old whiskey jug and put it on display. (A sprag pole is a piece of heavy timber supporting a mine ceiling.) Now operated by a nonprofit group, the museum has twelve exhibits on all aspects of the old town's history. One of those exhibits deals with Murray's most famous character: Molly B'Damn.

A Good-Hearted Woman

Born **Margaret Hall**, she arrived in New York from Ireland around 1873. Although the attractive, well-educated twenty-year-old could recite Shakespeare, to make a living she worked as a barmaid. That's how she met and married a young rake who lived off his family's money. When his father disowned him for marrying below his station, he quickly ran out of funds and forced Hall into prostitution. After a few years she quit her husband, but not her occupation. Known professionally as Molly, she made a good living mining miners and other boomtown denizens across the West.

When she heard of the gold strike in Idaho, Molly left for the new diggings. Getting as close to the new town as she could by train, she bought a horse and joined a pack train headed for Murray. On the way there, a severe blizzard struck. As they plodded on, a cold and exhausted young mother with a small child declared she could go no farther. Well dressed and traveling with ample furs, Molly told the train to go on, and she stayed behind, keeping mother and child warm in a makeshift shelter until the storm abated. When Molly made it to town with her two charges, she was hailed as a hero. At the time, she went by her former husband's name, which was Burdan. Her Irish brogue made "Burdan" sound like "B'Damn," so miners adopted that pronunciation.

Despite her occupation, Molly B'Damn endeared herself to the townspeople in Murray by helping the down-and-out. When she helped nurse sick miners and their families during a smallpox outbreak, she achieved near sainthood in the minds of locals. Molly survived the epidemic but died of "galloping consumption"—tuberculosis—in 1888.

Margaret Hall (1853–1888) is buried in **Murray Cemetery** (GPS coordinates: N47° 37.45', W115° 51.89'). More than 130 years after her death, the town remembers her with its annual Molly B'Damn Gold Rush Days celebration.

PIERCE (CLEARWATER COUNTY)

Elias Davidson Pierce (1824–1897) nearly died in the Mexican-American War—but from dysentery, not enemy fire. After the war he traveled to California during the 1849 Gold Rush. Pierce spent the 1850s in California, but, hoping for another bonanza, he began prospecting in Washington Territory. There, in October 1860, he and a partner found gold in Orofino Creek, in what is now northern Idaho. The mining camp that developed about a mile south of his claim was named Pierce in his honor. It became the seat of Shoshone County in early 1861. A log courthouse built in 1862 remained in use until 1885, when the county seat was moved to Murray. Pierce is now in Clearwater County.

When a lightning-laced thunderstorm blew into Pierce on the night of September 9, 1885, strings of firecrackers began popping along Main Street. The local Chinese had set them off in the belief they frightened away evil spirits. No one noticed that one of the reports was much louder than the others. Evil had not been entirely kept at bay.

The next morning, local merchant David M. Fraser was found dead in bed at the back of his Main Street store. He had been shot in the mouth and mutilated with a knife and an ax.

Seven Chinese men arrested for the murder were being escorted to the county seat in Murray on September 18 when a group of masked men stopped the party outside town. The vigilantes released two older men but lynched the other five.

Fraser's (1825–1885) grave is in **Normal Hill Cemetery** (1122 Seventh St., Lewiston; 208-746-6857). The five Chinese men were buried in Pierce's Chinese cemetery, but their bones were later exhumed and returned to their homeland, as was Chinese custom.

The restored Pierce courthouse, the state's oldest public building, still stands at Court Street and 1st Avenue, managed by the **J. Howard Bradbury Memorial Logging Museum** (208-464-2677).

POCATELLO (BANNOCK COUNTY)

Named for Shoshone chief Pocatello, the town was not founded until 1882—and another six years would pass before it was platted—but the general area had long been the heartland of the Shoshone-Bannock peoples, and later, a waypoint along the Oregon Trail. Emigrants had to get their wagons through Portneuf Gap, south of present-day Pocatello. The gap came to be called the Gateway, which inspired the town's later adoption of the term "Gateway to the Northwest" as its slogan. Pocatello gained a railroad connection in 1878 and another line four years later. With the discovery of gold and silver in Idaho Territory, the town saw heavy traffic and benefited economically. The town continued to grow as a railroad crossroads, and an educational, agricultural, and commercial center.

The downtown historic district covers eighteen blocks. **Historic Downtown Pocatello** (420 North Main St.; 208-232-7545) has a map showing the location of vintage buildings. Twenty-five Pocatello structures are listed on the National Register of Historic Places, and there are four National Register Historic Districts.

Nathaniel Wyeth came from Massachusetts in 1834 to establish a trading post on the Snake River he called **Fort Hall**. Three years later he sold out to Hudson's Bay Company, and the property went under British control. The new owners strengthened the fort's timber stockade with adobe and whitewashed it, making the post a gleaming landmark in the middle of nowhere. For emigrants on the Oregon Trail, Fort Hall was just about the last place to resupply and rest before undertaking the hardest part of the trail. When over-trapping and a big decline in the beaver hat market ended the fur trade, the trading post continued to cater to travelers along the Oregon Trail until it closed in 1855.

Nothing survives of the old trading post, or a second Fort Hall later built by the army on the Shoshone-Bannock Reservation. A 1962 reconstruction of the trading post, based on historical research, stands on the grounds of the **Bannock County Historical Museum** (3000 Avenue of the Chiefs; 208-233-0434).

In 1868, by the Fort Bridger Treaty, the Shoshone and Bannock peoples (collectively known as the Northern Paiute) agreed to live on a 1.8 million–acre reservation set aside for them in eastern Idaho. Later reduced in size to roughly 550,000 acres, the reservation is home to some six thousand tribal members. The **Shoshone-Bannock Tribal Museum** (30 East Ross Fork Rd.; 208-237-9791) tells the story of the two Fort Halls, the Shoshone-Bannock people, and their reservation.

Buffalo Horn

A Bannock war chief, **Buffalo Horn** (ca. 1825–1878), served as a scout under General Oliver O. Howard in the military's 1877 campaign against the Nez Perce. Earlier, the chief had ridden for a time as a scout for George Armstrong Custer, prior to Custer's demise at the Battle of the Little Big Horn. While Buffalo Horn had been willing to assist the US Army, his people came first. Provoked by the agricultural practices of newly arrived settlers—particularly the grazing of their livestock across a large area of camas roots that were one of his tribe's principal food sources—Buffalo Horn began attacking settlers. This led to what came to be called the Bannock-Paiute War, though it was only a bloody subset of the long clash of cultures between American Indians and Euro-Americans during the period of western expansion. The chief was mortally wounded in a clash with volunteer troops from Silver City, Idaho, in June 1878.

Buffalo Horn is buried in **Good Shepherd Cemetery**, Fort Hall (GPS coordinates: N43° 01.56', W112° 25.59'), but his journey to the grave was long. After his death, one of the militia members found his remains—or at least his head—and kept it as a souvenir. In 1914, the skull was donated to the Idaho State Historical Society, which held it until 1997, when it was returned to the Shoshone-Bannock Tribe and subsequently buried on their reservation.

SALMON (LEMHI COUNTY)

Long before the settlement of this mountain-flanked town at the junction of the Salmon and Lemhi Rivers, on August 11, 1805, the Lewis and Clark Expedition crossed the Continental Divide at 7,373-foot Lemhi Pass, about thirty miles southwest of what is now Salmon.

On the other side of the pass, the members of the Corps of Discovery raised the US flag—with all of fifteen stars—for the first time west of the Rocky Mountains.

Serving as a guide and translator for the expedition was a Sho-shone woman known as Sacajawea. A mile east of town on State Highway 28, the **Sacajawea Interpretive, Cultural, and Educational Center** (2700 Main St.; 208-756-1188) has interpretive exhibits and a self-guided, mile-long outdoor interpretive trail. The center is located on a seventy-one-acre park that features a bronze statue of Sacajawea holding her baby. Sculpted by Agnes Vincen Talbot, the artwork was dedicated in 2005.

The town was founded in 1867 by George L. Shoup, a merchant who had come to the area from Virginia City in Montana Territory following the discovery of gold in the area the year before. He made a good living supplying miners, and went on to do even better in the land and cattle business. He later served as Idaho's final territorial governor, and following statehood in 1890, he became one of its first two US senators.

The history of the town and county is the focus of the **Lemhi County Museum** (210 Main St.; 208-756-3342). The museum features a large collection of Shoshone artifacts, as well as exhibits related to the Gold Rush era, Chinese workers, and ranching.

Leesburg Ghost Town

Thirty-two miles northwest of Salmon is the ghost town of Lees-burg. Named for Confederate general Robert E. Lee, it was set-tled in 1866 following prospector Frank Sharkey's discovery of placer gold in nearby creeks. With sectional feelings still running strong after the Civil War, pro-Union miners established their own camp—Grantsville—adjacent to Leesburg, but in this contest the Southerners prevailed. Grantsville was soon overrun by Leesburg. The mining camp became a boomtown, with a population of three thousand. Placer mining, followed by hard-rock mining, produced some $40 million in gold before the precious metal bearing ore was played out in the early 1940s. But the town had peaked long before then. Today about fifteen old buildings still stand at the still-remote site. Interpretive signs tell the once-upon-a-time town's story. An old cemetery is a short walk from there.

SILVER CITY (OWYHEE COUNTY)

Mining activity that would lead to the development of Silver City began when prospectors found placer gold in the Owyhee Mountains of southwestern Idaho in May 1863. But in midsummer that year, rich deposits of silver ore were discovered. Founded in 1864, during its peak boom years Silver City had seventy-five businesses and three hundred residences, as well as a dozen ore-processing mills. The town got another economic boost when it became the county seat in 1866. It saw two intense periods of violent disputes over mining claim boundaries, the second so bad that the governor had to send in troops to restore order.

Served by several stagecoach lines, with a top population of four thousand, the town was the first in Idaho to have a telegraph connection and the first to support a daily newspaper. By the early 1880s the town had telephones, and in the early 1900s, electricity.

Though hundreds of mines once operated in the area, one by one they fizzled out. While they lasted, they produced an estimated $60 million in gold and silver. In 1934, the town lost its county seat status, and soon only a few residences and businesses remained. A new open pit mine, one of the nation's largest, began operation in 1977, but closed in 2000.

Not only is Silver City considered Idaho's best-preserved ghost town, it's also one of the more intact of any of the ghost towns in the West. Two factors lie behind that. First, at its high point, it was a substantial city, not just a small mining camp. Second, unlike so many other boomtowns, Silver City never had a devastating fire. Nor has it become overly commercialized. The Silver City Historic District is listed on the National Register of Historic Places, and the town is on federal Bureau of Land Management land.

The ghost town is thirty-seven miles southwest of Boise. From Boise take I-84 west to Nampa, then drive south on State Highway 45 and then east on State Highway 78, to Silver City Road. Follow Silver City Road 19.9 miles to Washington Street, the town's main thoroughfare.

The two-story, wood-frame former schoolhouse, built in 1892 and used until 1932, houses a local history museum that's open during the summer months. In Murphy, about twenty-four miles from Silver City, the **Idaho Hotel** (P.O. Box 75; 208-583-4104), built in 1863 and expanded with a three-story wing in 1866, reopened to summer guests in 1972.

SODA SPRINGS (CARIBOU COUNTY)

While today a case of bottled mineral water is no farther away than the closest grocery store, the naturally carbonated springs that gave this town its name were a favorite stopping place for travelers along the Oregon Trail. Pioneers drank the bubbly water straight, put sugar in it, flavored it with lemon extract, and even used it in baking bread; whatever way they chose, they considered it a wonderful wilderness treat.

Roughly six miles west of Soda Springs was the Hudspeth Cutoff, named for Benoni M. Hudspeth, who in the summer of 1849 blazed a new trail that branched from the Oregon Trail to the California gold-fields. A historical marker at the junction of US 30 and State Highway 34 stands near the cutoff.

The army established a fort near the springs in 1863. The post did not remain garrisoned for long, and a party of Mormons settled in the vicinity for a time, but the community of Soda Springs dates from the 1870 discovery of gold in the area by Canadian-born Jesse "Caribou Jack" Fairchild, the namesake of the county. The strike led to the extraction of an estimated $50 million in placer gold before it petered out twenty years later.

Wagon Box Grave

The cool mineral springs were as welcome to West-bound travelers as the threat of attack by American Indians along the trail was worrying. In the summer of 1861, a family of seven stopped for the night not far from the springs. As they slept, their wagon team strayed. In the morning, the family stayed behind to look for their horses while the other wagons in their party moved on. When another wagon train reached the springs the next day, they found that all seven of the stragglers, a couple and their five children, had been killed by Indians.

Traveler George Goodheart described what happened next:

> We then covered them all up with quilts and took the upper sideboards and sawed them so they would fit across the wagon box. We put some across over the old Folks' faces and some over the children's faces at the foot. They we got some willows from Soda Creek and cut them so as to cover the whole length of the wagon box. We then spread quilts over them, covered them with dirt, and set four formation rocks, one at each corner.

A substantial gray granite marker donated in 1934 by Bott Brothers Monument Works in Logan, Utah, stands near the entrance to **Fairview Cemetery** (West Center St. at South First St. West) in the vicinity of the mass burial. The site came to be known as the Wagon Box Grave.

Also in the cemetery is the final resting place of prospector Jesse "Caribou Jack" Fairchild (1836–1881). The grave is located in the center of the cemetery, marked with a pink granite monument placed in the twentieth century.

WALLACE (SHOSHONE COUNTY)

Founded in 1884 during Idaho's silver-mining boom days, the town suffered a devastating fire in 1910, although two-thirds of its late-Victorian architecture survived. Known as the Silver Capital of the World, Wallace's area mines have produced more than 1.2 billion ounces of the precious metal. The entire town of Wallace is on the National Register of Historic Places.

Occupying the old Rice's Bakery, the **Wallace District Mining Museum** (509 Bank St.; 208-556-1592) focuses on the area's rich mining history, as well as Wallace and the 1910 fire, known locally as the Big Burn.

Railroads first reached the Coeur d'Alene Mining District in 1887, and Wallace's Northern Pacific Railroad depot was built in 1901, with bricks shipped in from Tacoma, Washington, and concrete panels made from repurposed mine tailings. The chateau-style depot did its own traveling in 1986, when Interstate 90 was under construction. Contractors moved the historic depot two hundred feet across the Coeur d'Alene River to its current location, where today the **Northern Pacific Depot Museum** (219 Sixth St.; 208-752-0111) houses exhibits dedicated to local history.

Known as the Bi-Metallic Building, this structure started out in 1895 as a hotel and saloon, but later became another kind of accommodation—one for ladies of the evening (or any other time, for that matter). One of five houses of prostitution in Wallace during its boisterous heyday, the **Oasis Bordello** (1605 Cedar St.; 208-753-0801) is now a museum dedicated to the story of the shady ladies who plied their trade here and elsewhere across the Wild West.

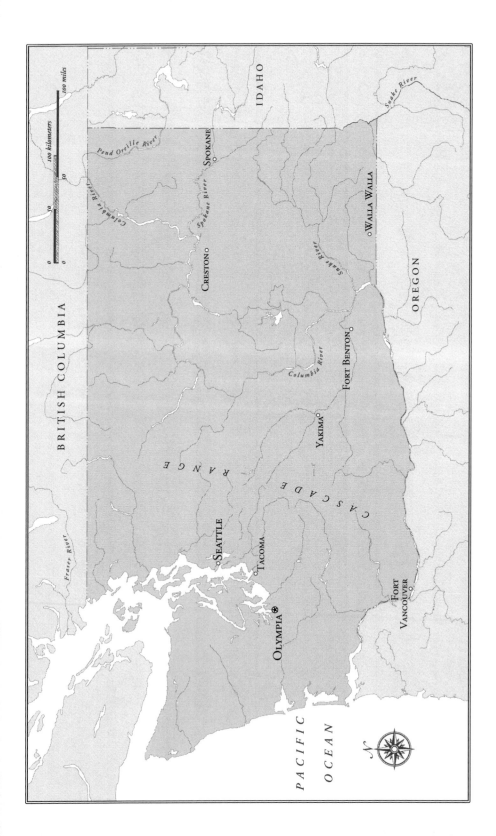

WASHINGTON

BELLINGHAM (WHATCOM COUNTY)

Two California men set up a sawmill in 1852 where Whatcom Creek flows into Puget Sound. Other settlers followed, and soon four different communities had sprung up—Whatcom, New Whatcom, Fairhaven, and Sehome. They were combined in 1904 to form Bellingham. For a time, Bellingham was Washington's fourth-largest city. Loggers and commercial fishermen kept the place lively in its early years.

Whatcom Museum of History and Art (121 Prospect St.; 360-778-8930) is housed in the old city hall built in 1892. The museum opened in 1940. The **Lynden Pioneer Museum** (217 Front St., Lynden; 360-354-3675) is fourteen miles north of Bellingham.

CENTRALIA (LEWIS COUNTY)

The son of an enslaved Virginia man, George Washington founded Centralia in 1875. He traveled west on the Oregon Trail in 1850 with the white couple who had raised him, Anna and James Cochran. Washington and the Cochrans came in search of a new beginning, and they found it. Initially, they settled in Oregon City, Oregon, but later they crossed the Columbia River into what soon became Washington Territory.

Lewis County Historical Museum (599 Northwest Front Way; 360-748-0831) is housed in the 1912-vintage Burlington Northern Railroad Depot.

For Sale: Sturdy Fort, Never Used

During the Washington State Indian Wars in 1856, Captain Francis Goff and five men of the Oregon Volunteers built a two-story log blockhouse to guard the Chehalis River crossing and as a place to store supplies. Either the fortification intimidated the hostiles, or they did not think it important enough to attack, but the blockhouse never saw any fighting. After the war, settler Joseph Borst bought the structure for $500 and used it as a granary. It remained on its original site until 1919, when it was moved to Riverside Park in Centralia. Two years later, it was moved to its current location at **Borst Park** (West of I-5, off exit 82), a 121-acre recreation area. Standing near the old fort is the **Borst Home**, a two-story frame Greek Revival–style mansion built in 1857.

COLFAX (WHITMAN COUNTY)

In 1870, twenty-nine-year-old James A. Perkins and another man set up a sawmill along the South Fork of the Palouse River in southeastern Washington. They built a log cabin, the beginning of the community that became Colfax. The partner soon decided to leave, but Perkins took on a new partner and stayed.

Perkins and his new associate surveyed a townsite in the spring of 1871, which Perkins named Belleville. The same year, Perkins married Sarah Jane (Jennie) Ewert. Their marriage would endure, but as the town grew, Jennie chafed at its name. While most historians believe Perkins named the town for his native Belleville, Illinois, Jennie thought it honored a former girlfriend. A man smart enough to start his own town was also smart enough not to argue the point, and he renamed the community Colfax, in honor of Ulysses S. Grant's vice president, Schuyler Colfax.

By 1889, Colfax was a thriving county-seat town in need of a new courthouse. Taxpayers funded an impressive, two-story "temple of justice" meant to be the symbol of law and order for Whitman County. But not everything that transpired in it was lawful or orderly.

In the spring of 1894, two accused killers were cooling their heels in the county jail in the courthouse basement. One was awaiting trial, while the other was soon to be released after having been convicted of a lesser crime. In the predawn hours of June 1, someone knocked on the jail's door. When the jailer opened it, a mob overpowered him and dragged the two prisoners to the upstairs courtroom. There, nooses were placed around their necks and they were tossed off the second-floor balcony to strangle.

It's not really true that lightning doesn't strike twice. In 1898, two men languished in the same jail, accused of killing a man in a robbery elsewhere in the county. As had happened four years before, armed men stormed the hoosegow, intent on lynching both prisoners. They succeeded in throwing one from the second floor, and like the pair lynched in 1894, he died by strangulation. But the other prisoner had stuffed cloth in the keyhole of his cell door, and before the mob could figure out how to unlock it, the sheriff showed up and restored order.

The old courthouse, scene of three gruesome extralegal hangings, was torn down in 1957. But visitors can learn more about the three Colfax lynchings at the **Perkins House Museum** (623 North Perkins Ave.; 509-397-2555). Operated by the Whitman County Historical Society, the museum is in the two-story Victorian home of the town's founder, built in 1886.

An Old West Tourist Attraction

Rising 3,612 feet above sea level, **Steptoe Butte** affords a commanding view of the surrounding countryside in southeastern Washington. First known as Pyramid Peak, it was renamed in honor of Colonel Edward Steptoe. Nearly twenty years after the Battle of Rosalia (see Rosalia, Washington), with Washington State's Indian Wars long over, James S. "Cashup" Davis acquired Steptoe Butte from the Northern Pacific Railroad and cleared a wagon road to its summit. In 1888, he built a two-story frame hotel on top of the butte. Given the impressive view, he envisioned his property as a resort destination. To add to the place's attraction, on top of the hotel he built a glass observatory with a telescope. Due to its remoteness, the Cashup Hotel never did very well, but Davis and his wife continued to live there until her death in 1894, and his in 1896. The hotel burned down in 1911. The State of Washington acquired the butte and surrounding land by donation and opened the 136-acre **Steptoe Butte State Park Heritage Site** (Hume Rd.; 509-337-6457) in 1946.

COUPEVILLE (ISLAND COUNTY)

Weighing anchor on his former life as a sea captain, Thomas Coupe settled Washington's second-oldest community in 1852. In the days of sailing ships, life on the ocean could never be taken for granted, and neither could a pioneer's likelihood of longevity in Indian territory. Isaac Ebey, who had settled on Whidbey Island two years before Coupe arrived, was killed by Indians in 1857. But Coupe and others who followed him persevered, and he became the town's namesake.

Island County Historical Museum (908 Northwest Alexander St.; 360-678-3310) curates artifacts ranging from American Indian cultural items to relics illustrating the later history and culture of the county.

The **Ebey's Landing National Historical Reserve** encompasses twenty-five square miles of history, including one hundred structures listed on the National Register of Historic Places. The reserve's visitor center (162 Cemetery Rd.; 360-678-6084) is two miles west of Coupeville off State Highway 20.

DAVENPORT (LINCOLN COUNTY)

A small agricultural community in northeastern Washington, Davenport was founded in 1883 by John C. Davenport near a spring that had long been used by American Indians and later by miners headed to the goldfields in western Montana.

The bloody flight of escaped Oregon State Penitentiary inmate Harry Tracy (see Salem, Oregon) ended in a field near Davenport on August 5, 1902. After sustaining two serious gunshot wounds when cornered by a posse, Tracy killed himself.

Opened in 1972, the **Lincoln County Historical Museum** (600 Seventh St.; 509-725-6711) has an exhibit on Tracy, including several items recovered from the dead outlaw's body.

DAYTON (COLUMBIA COUNTY)

The area's first settlers arrived in the mid-1850s, and in the following decade a small farming town had developed. Named for Jesse N. Day, this community on the Touchet River just beyond the foothills of the Blue Mountains did not really take off until the railroad arrived. Like most towns that boomed with the arrival of rail service, Dayton developed a lively saloon and red-light district. The vice dens are long gone, but the town has three historic districts, with 150-plus structures listed on the National Register of Historic Places.

"Land Jumping" Frowned On

"Land jumping" was the term applied to squatting on real estate not your own. Understandably, property owners took exception to land jumpers. In 1878, a group of farmers organized as the Settlers' Protection Committee called on one J. N. Sparks and told him to vacate the property on which he had been squatting. He declined. Not long after, when a committee member's son forced Sparks off a downtown boardwalk and a crowd gathered, Sparks pulled a pistol and started shooting in their general direction. He was deliberately shooting low, evidently hoping to scare off his antagonists. Some of the committee members, however, did not shoot low. Sparks caught a bullet in his cheek and one in his neck. The committee discussed lynching him but did not proceed. As soon as he got well enough to travel, Sparks left the county, and the committee issued a notice that no further land jumping would be tolerated.

Washington's oldest surviving railroad depot, the **Dayton Historic Depot**, was constructed in 1881 by the Oregon Railway and Navigation Company. A second rail line reached the town in 1889 and it also used the depot. Ten years later, the Union Pacific Railroad (which had acquired the two smaller lines) moved the depot to a new location by jacking it up, placing it on logs, and pulling it by horse teams. The depot continued in operation until 1971. Ten years later, it reopened as a museum (222 Commercial St.; 509-382-2026) dedicated to Dayton and Columbia County history.

ILWACO (PACIFIC COUNTY)

Meriwether Lewis, William Clark, and their Corps of Discovery camped at this point at the mouth of the Columbia River in November 1805 shortly after Clark had his first glimpse of the Pacific Ocean. Americans began settling in the area in the 1840s.

A part of the Washington state park system, the **Lewis and Clark Interpretive Center** (244 Robert Gray Dr.; 360-642-3029) offers an overview of the Lewis and Clark Expedition and the maritime history of the area. The center is located on the grounds of Cape Disappointment State Park (formerly Fort Canby).

First known as the Ilwaco Heritage Center, the **Columbia Pacific Heritage Museum** (115 Southeast Lake St.; 360-642-3446) began in the early 1980s in a building vacated by a locally owned telephone company after it was absorbed by a larger provider. The driving force behind the museum was then Ilwaco city council member Noreen Robinson, who helped raise money for it by selling hot dogs at local events. The original museum building was remodeled and expanded in 1990 and now houses more than 23,000 artifacts, documents, and photographs.

NEWPORT (PEND OREILLE COUNTY)

Just across the Pend Oreille River from Idaho, Newport was founded in 1890 as a new port—hence the name—to accommodate the first steamboats to ply the waterway. When the Great Northern Railroad came through in 1892, Newport became a mining and timber industry shipping point. The riverboat era did not end here until 1927, later than most places in the West, with the completion of the Pend Oreille River Bridge.

What did not come to an end was the Koch Saloon, first known as the Newport Club. John Koch opened it in 1894, importing an ornate bar-back furnishing that came around Cape Horn to the Washington coast. The watering hole remains in business as **Kelly's Bar & Grill** (324 West 4th St.; 509-447-3267), and is the second-oldest bar in the state.

Learn more local and area history at the **Pend Oreille County Historical Museum** (402 South Washington Ave.; 509-447-5388). Housed in the two-story Idaho and Northern Washington Railroad depot, built in 1908, the museum is part of a complex that includes three restored vintage log cabins that were moved to the property from their original locations.

OLYMPIA (THURSTON COUNTY)

Olympia was named Washington's territorial capital in 1853 and remained the seat of government following statehood in 1889. Being on the southern tip of Puget Sound, the city became a busy port during the nineteenth century, and the pace only picked up when Olympia gained railroad connections.

A self-guided walking tour prepared by the Olympia Heritage Commission listing thirty downtown historic sites of interest is available at the **State Capitol Visitor Information Center** (14th St. and Capital Way South; 360-586-3460). The history of Olympia is documented at the **Bigelow House Museum** (918 Glass Ave. NE; 360-753-1215). Olympia attorney Daniel Bigelow, who traveled the Oregon Trail in 1851, built the house in 1854.

Opened in 1892 as the Thurston County courthouse, the stone building (1110 Capitol Way South) became Washington's capitol in 1905. The building housed the state's legislature and other govern-mental offices until the present capitol came into use in 1928. The tenacious structure survived a major fire that destroyed a central tower in 1928 and a powerful earthquake in 1949 that claimed more of its turret-like towers. Still an impressive building, the **old Washington capitol** houses the offices of the state's education agency.

Omak (Okanogan County)

Omak was not founded until 1907, but it lies at the western edge of the 2.8-million-acre Colville Indian Reservation where Nez Perce Chief Joseph spent his final years. Created in 1872, the reservation is the home of the Colville Confederated Tribes, twelve bands that include the Chelan, Chief Joseph Band of Nez Perce, Colville, Eniat, Lakes, Methow, Moses-Columbia, Nespelem, Okanogan, Palus, San Poil, and Wenatchi.

Four miles southeast of Omak, the culture of these people is documented at the **Colville Confederated Tribes Museum** (512 Mead Way, Coulee Dam, Washington; 509-633-0751).

"My heart is sick and sad."

The words Chief Joseph spoke when he surrendered continue to resonate: *Hear me, my chiefs! I am tired. My heart is sick and sad. From where the sun now stands, I will fight no more forever.*

The chief and what remained of his tribe were allowed in 1885 to move to the Colville Indian Reservation from Indian Territory in what is now Oklahoma. For the rest of his life, Joseph continued his appeals to the government in hopes of being able to return his people to their homeland. He died in 1904 in what he perceived as exile, and was buried in the **Colville Indian Cemetery**. A memorial dedicated to Chief Joseph stands off Route 155 in Nespelem, thirty-six miles southwest of Omak.

Port Townsend (Jefferson County)

First settled in 1851, Port Townsend seemed destined to become a major city, perhaps the "New York" of the West Coast. Given its location on upper Puget Sound, all it needed was a transcontinental railroad connection to become a great Pacific seaport. But Tacoma, and not long after, Seattle, got the railroad instead. While that stunted the town's growth, it did not kill it. Not having boomed, the city still has most of its original Victorian architecture.

Built in 1889 by retired sea captain (and onetime county sheriff) Henry L. Tibbals, this three-story brick structure, a striking example of the Richardson Romanesque architectural style, has accommodated a variety of businesses over the years. Among other enterprises, it has been used as a saloon, billiard parlor, theater, newspaper, and brothel known as the "Palace of Sweets." Following extensive restoration from 1976 to 1984, the building opened as the **Palace Hotel** (1004 Water St.; 360-385-0773).

Curated by the Jefferson County Historical Society, the **Jefferson County Historical Museum** (540 Water St.; 360-385-1003) is in the 1892-vintage former city hall. In addition to city offices, the building once housed the police department and jail. Exhibits cover the city and county's history and spotlight two cultures that contributed significantly to the area's rich heritage—the Hoh, S'Klallam and Chimacum Tribes, and the Chinese community.

Looked for Love in All the Wrong Places

Port Townsend was also the home base for Missouri-born outlaw **Jake Terry**. His criminal career spanned more than three decades, beginning in 1873 with a saloon shooting in Seattle and ending in the US–Canadian border town of Sumas in 1907. Terry—folks called him "Cowboy"—specialized in smuggling Chinese laborers into the United States, along with opium. But he was wanted for assault to murder, and suspected of more serious crimes, when he showed up in Sumas as the small town celebrated the Fourth of July. What tripped him up was love—or lust.

Earlier, doing time at San Quentin in the 1890s, he had met stagecoach robber Bill Miner, and following their release from prison they teamed up to pull off Canada's first-ever train robbery in 1904. They followed that up with another train robbery near Portland, Oregon, a year later, then split up. Given Terry's lengthy rap sheet, it would seem logical that he would spend the rest of his days in prison or get killed in a shoot-out with law enforcement. But when Terry tried to rekindle a relationship with his ex-wife, who operated a confectionery in Sumas, Annie's new husband Gus Lindsey naturally objected. This led to a gun-fight with Lindsey and some of his friends, although none of the participants was hit. Charged with assault with intent to murder, Terry fled to Canada.

Eighteen months later, still pining for his former wife (who reportedly had not discouraged his efforts), Terry went to her house on July 5, 1907. Around noon, Lindsey came home for lunch to find Terry about to walk into his bedroom. He shot the interloper twice in the head with a .38 caliber revolver, and, as the newspapers put it, the outlaw fell dead "with a curse on his lips." Terry's body was carried to a hardware store where a doctor obligingly performed an autopsy in the storeroom window for all to see. After that, the outlaw's remains—minus the finger some-one had cut off while stealing a fourteen-carat gold ring he didn't need anymore—were shipped to the county seat at Bellingham for burial.

Terry's grave lies in **Bayview Cemetery** (1420 Woburn St., Bellingham; 360-778-7150). Located in a former Methodist Church parsonage, the **Sumas Historical Museum** (114 Second St.; 360-988-0322) tells the story of Sumas, a once-rowdy bor-der town and smuggling enclave. Loggers, trappers, and later, gold miners, often whooped it up here, and "Cowboy" Terry got his while looking for love in all the wrong places.

PUYALLUP (PIERCE COUNTY)

The founder of Puyallup lived to be nearly a hundred and never lost his pioneer spirit. In 1852, with his wife and infant son, Ezra Meeker (1830–1928) spent five hard months traveling westward along the Oregon Trail in an ox-drawn covered wagon. Initially settling in the Portland vicinity, with the development of Washington Territory he moved to Puget Sound. There Meeker plotted the town of Puyallup and served as its first mayor. He made a fortune cultivating hops (in the process developing a world demand for it), went bust when an insect infestation destroyed that market for a time, and grew wealthy again as a vegetable farmer and businessman.

Through his writing, lectures, and what would come to be called publicity stunts, Meeker spent the last two decades of his life promoting the history of America's westward movement. At seventy-six, Meeker drove an ox-drawn covered wagon along the old Oregon Trail to push for marking the route. He did it again four years later, and later still flew over the trail with army aviator Lieutenant Oakley Kelley. Meeker died not long after embarking on his fifth trip along the old trail, this time by automobile. His efforts paid off, as the Oregon Trail is one of the nation's best-known, -preserved, and -marked historic transportation arteries.

In 1886, Meeker began building a two-story mansion in Puyallup. The seventeen-room, Italianate Victorian house was completed in 1890 and remained in the family until 1912. Later it was used as a home for Civil War widows, a hospital, and a nursing home. In 1970 the old **Ezra Meeker Mansion** (312 Spring St.; 253-848-1770) was restored and opened to the public. Operated by the Puyallup Historical Society, its exhibits focus on Meeker's influence on Puyallup and his efforts to keep the history of the Old West alive.

ROSALIA (WHITMAN COUNTY)

Located near the Washington–Idaho border, this small town was founded in 1870 by T. J. Favorite, who named the community for his wife. Another twenty-four years would pass before the town's incorporation in 1894.

Colonel Edward J. Steptoe's (1816–1865) name is little-known today, but if not for his military prowess, and a little luck, he'd be remembered for losing his entire command, just like George Armstrong Custer would do eighteen years later in Montana.

On May 16, 1858, a large party of Coeur d'Alene, Cayuse, Palouse, Spokane, and Yakama warriors confronted and began harassing Steptoe's column of 158 Ninth Infantry dragoons. On their way from Fort Walla Walla to Fort Colfax, the colonel and his troops made camp for the night. Later that evening, a delegation of chiefs approached and told Steptoe he could march no farther on their land. Vastly outnumbered by an estimated eight hundred to one thousand warriors, the colonel realized his only hope would be to return to Fort Walla Walla.

In the morning, as Steptoe began to withdraw, the Indians attacked. This began a running battle that lasted for most of the day. When the command came to high ground near present-day Rosalia, Washington, Steptoe ordered his soldiers to take position for a last stand. Fighting continued until nightfall. The Indians intended to make a final assault in the morning, but during the night Steptoe succeeded in escaping. If the Indians had pressed their advantage, with the soldiers almost out of ammunition, the command would have been overwhelmed. As it was, Steptoe lost only seven men and killed nine of the attackers, with some two score Indians wounded. The fight came to be called the **Battle of Rosalia**.

A granite monument commemorating the battle was erected by the Daughters of the American Revolution in 1914, on a hill in a four-acre state park (South Summit Loop; 509-337-6457). What could have been Steptoe's Last Stand took place just to the southwest, where Rosalia High School's football field is now located.

SEATTLE (KING COUNTY)

From its founding in 1851, Seattle grew from a single log cabin to a robust frontier city built on logging and the commercial fishing industry, in just two decades. The city was named in honor of Duwamish chief Sealth, who warmly welcomed early settlers and saw to it that peaceful relations prevailed between his people and the whites. But four years later, hostilities would erupt between the new arrivals and other indigenous peoples of the Pacific Northwest.

A band of Nisqually warriors under Chief Leschi attacked the frontier settlement on January 26, 1856, during the 1855–1856

Yakama War. Friendly Indians had warned settlers of the impending action, which likely saved many lives. In one of the more unusual engagements of the Indian Wars, a US Navy sloop-of-war, the USS *Decatur*, used its thirty-two-pound guns on the Nisqually and thwarted the attack.

Decatur High School in Federal Way, a city in the metropolitan Seattle area, was named for the ship that saved Seattle from being overrun by hostile Indians. The ship continued in active service through the Civil War before being sold by the navy in San Francisco, in 1865. Its fate after that is unknown. In 1912, a statue honoring Chief Sealth (more commonly known by the Anglicized name "Seattle") was dedicated at what is now the intersection of Fifth Avenue, Denny Way, and Cedar Street, Seattle. The chief stands with his right arm raised in welcome.

The eighteen-block area known as **Pioneer Square** was the economic center of early-day Seattle. As was not uncommon in the Wild West, a disastrous fire destroyed most of the business district in 1889. That catastrophe prompted property owners to rebuild with brick and mortar, and many of those Victorian-era structures still stand throughout downtown.

With the discovery of gold in the Yukon in 1897, the seaport became the principal point of departure for fortune seekers headed north to Canada's Yukon Territory and US-owned Alaska.

The Seattle unit of the **Klondike Gold Rush National Historical Park** (319 Second Ave. South; 206-220-4240) is in the old Cadillac Hotel, built in 1889. The hotel saw a lot of business during the Klondike Gold Rush stampede. The visitor's center and museum opened in 1979 in another early-day Seattle building, but later moved to its current location. The facility was heavily damaged in the 2001 Nisqually earthquake and did not reopen until rehabilitation was completed five years later. The other unit of this park is located in Alaska (see Skagway, Alaska).

George Washington Carmack (1860–1922), the man credited with the discovery that set off the great Klondike Gold Rush of

1897–1899 is buried in **Evergreen Washelli Memorial Park** (11111 Aurora Ave. North; 206-362-5200). Having made a fortune from his claim, Carmack left Alaska for Hollister, California, where he established a large ranch. In 1900, he moved to Seattle, where he spent the rest of his life. Carmack's flat tombstone is in Section F, Lot 0077, Grave 5A.

Former Seattle lawman Joel F. Warren (1858–1933) is also buried in Evergreen Washelli Memorial Park.

When Warren was appointed Seattle's police chief in 1917, the city gained the services of a veteran Old West lawman who one newspaper noted had been shot at—and missed—thirteen times. Absent from the article reporting the number of Warren's close calls was any mention of how many men he'd shot in the line of duty. The piece only noted that he had "put a few notches in his own gun to demonstrate his marksmanship."

Born in Missouri, Warren came to Washington in 1865 with his family. They settled in Walla Walla, but in 1879 they drove a herd of cattle to Spokane, liked what they saw, and stayed. Warren's parents claimed 160 acres in still mostly rural Spokane County under the 1862 Homestead Act, and Warren filed on an additional 160 acres.

Warren began his long career of public service in 1883 when he served as a deputy county tax assessor. The following year, the Spokane County sheriff offered a $50 reward for the arrest of one Bill Jackson, a wanted murderer. Warren rode into town and captured the outlaw. That netted an offer from impressed city officials to take on the job of city marshal, and Warren accepted. He served two separate stints, running a private detective agency between his terms as marshal.

In 1900, Warren went north to Alaska during the Klondike Gold Rush, and soon was serving as Nome's police chief. Back in the States after the boom went bust, he hired on as a federal agent. In 1915, he was part of the security team at the World's Fair in San Francisco. After serving as Seattle's police chief, he worked as a King County deputy sheriff until shortly before his death, at the age of seventy-six.

Spokane (Spokane County)

Named for the Spokane people, Spokane developed as "Spokan" (no "e" until 1883) Falls in 1873 with the construction of a sawmill that harnessed the power of the nearby Columbia River falls. The town boomed with the arrival of the Northern Pacific Railroad in 1881, followed by a transcontinental connection two years later. When rich deposits of gold were discovered in northern Idaho in 1884, Spokane became the gateway city to the Coeur d'Alene mining district. Even after the boom played out in Idaho, Spokane remained eastern Washington's transportation hub.

The downtown area includes three National Register Historic Districts, with fifteen historic districts elsewhere in the city, the most of any city in the state. The **Spokane Visitor Center** (620 West Spokane Falls Blvd.; 509-747-3230) offers a brochure with a self-guided walking tour of downtown Spokane historical sites. The **Northwest Museum of Arts and Culture** (2316 West First Ave.; 509-456-3931) has a large American Indian and regional history collection in addition to its other holdings, which range from art to archival material. Ten miles from downtown is the **Spokane Valley Museum** (12114 East Sprague Ave., Spokane Valley; 509-922-4570).

Washington's Indian Wars

In reprisal for the May 1858 attack on Colonel Edward J. Steptoe's column at present-day Rosalia, Washington, a command led by Colonel George Wright was ordered by General Newman Clarke to undertake a punitive campaign against the Indians who had attacked Steptoe's dragoons. The colonel engaged the Indians on September 1 that year. Wright fought the Indians again four days later in what became known as the **Battle of Spokane Plains**. Losing none of their own, Wright's expedition killed seventeen to twenty warriors and wounded another forty to fifty. A Depression-era monument on the site (1399 S. Dover Rd., Medical Lake) says that seven hundred army soldiers defeated "5,000 allied

Indians," but later research shows that both sides were evenly matched. The army fielded roughly five hundred soldiers, and the Indians had only slightly more than that.

The **Battle of Four Lakes** took place thirteen miles from present-day Spokane in the vicinity of 13219 W. 1st Avenue, Four Lakes. The Spokane County Pioneer Society placed a pyramid-shaped monument at the site in 1935.

In 1880 the US Army established Camp Spokane near the confluence of the Spokane and Columbia Rivers, twenty-three miles northwest of Spokane. The last frontier post established anywhere in the West, the post was designated a fort in 1882. Its primary mission was to maintain peace between area settlers and the tribes located at the sprawling Colville and Spokane Indian Reservations. The military abandoned Fort Spokane in 1898, its troops deployed to Cuba at the onset of the Spanish-American War. The post was converted to an Indian boarding school, which continued in operation until 1916, when the school closed and became a tuberculosis hospital for people living on the reservations.

When the hospital closed in 1929, the old fort stood vacant until the National Park Service acquired the site in 1960. With four of the original fort buildings still standing, the site is now part of the Lake Roosevelt National Recreation Area. The **Fort Spokane Visitor Center** (44150 District Office Ln., Davenport; 509-754-7800) is housed in the old fort's guardhouse and has interpretive exhibits on the history of the fort, the reservations, and the boarding school.

James Glispin is perhaps best known for having led the posse that captured the Younger brothers and killed Jesse James gang member Charlie Pitts near Madelia, Minnesota, following the botched 1876 Northfield Raid. Glispin also served three terms as Watonwan County sheriff before he and his wife moved to Spokane in 1883. He was elected city marshal of what was then called Spokane Falls on April 7, 1885, and appointed deputy US marshal in January 1886. The following April, Glispin was elected police chief. His final law enforcement job was as Spokane County sheriff from 1887 to 1888. While sheriff, he headed the posse that captured two men who had killed Spokane police officer Robert Rusk. Glispin (1846–1890) died of natural causes on November 23, 1890.

The former sheriff is buried in **Fairmount Memorial Park** (5200 W. Wellesley; 509-326-3800), next to his mother, Anathasia, who outlived him by four years. Mother and son share the same gravestone. In 2006, a stone monument relating his background and summarizing his career was placed near the graveside.

Butch Cassidy Didn't Sleep Here– But Who Did?

For years, the one-story, four-bedroom Craftsman-style house at 1001 Providence Avenue in Spokane's Garland District stood vacant, its windows shuttered. In the spring of 2018, Spokane investor Rick Tannehill bought the 1916-vintage structure, remodeled it, and got the property zoned as commercial. Not until he had closed on the house and begun its renovation did Tannehill learn that the old place came with a particularly intriguing story. Had one of the Wild West's best-known outlaws once lived there under an assumed name?

Born in Michigan in 1872 or 1873, William T. Phillips, his wife, and their son occupied the house from 1925 to 1932. A machine shop owner and well-regarded Elks Lodge member, Phillips had paid $5,000 for the house, big money at the time. But Phillips lost his business during the Great Depression and died broke in 1937, his ashes scattered by his widow over the Little Spokane River. All of that would be just another sad story connected to the nation's worst economic downturn were it not for the fact that for a time, based on a typescript called "Bandit Invincible" that he had written on his machine shop stationery, some people believed that Phillips was actually the outlaw Butch Cassidy. His manuscript, though amateurishly written and with ample errors of fact, did seem to indicate some firsthand knowledge of the outlaw's exploits.

Research by Cassidy experts, notably author-historian Dan Buck, has ruled Phillips out as Cassidy, who is believed to have been killed in Bolivia in 1908. But historians are pretty sure that Phillips was a Wyoming State Prison alum named William T. Wilcox. Wilcox had been in the Wyoming penitentiary at the same time Cassidy was behind bars there (1894–1896), and almost surely knew him. After doing two stretches for burglary and check forgery, Wilcox changed his name and reinvented himself. During the Depression, he apparently hoped to capitalize on his association with Cassidy. In fact, on a visit to Wyoming in the early 1930s, he claimed to be Cassidy, never mentioning anyone named Wilcox.

The Phillips house is privately owned but can be viewed from the street.

TACOMA (PIERCE COUNTY)

Tacoma's roots go back to the establishment of Fort Nisqually, built in 1833 as a Hudson's Bay Company trading post. The fort flourished as an international trading center until the market for beaver pelts and other furs declined. In the 1840s, at a second location, it served as the hub of an extensive farming operation. After Washington State became a US territory, the Hudson's Bay Company sold the fort's buildings to the federal government and left.

Originally located at nearby DuPont, Washington, the fort slowly deteriorated. By the 1930s only two of the original buildings remained—the granary and the factor's house. The federal Works Progress Administration reconstructed the fort at **Point Defiance Park** and the two historic structures were moved to the new location (5400 North Pearl St.). Built in 1843, the granary is the oldest building in Washington State.

Despite the early presence of a fort, nearly twenty years passed before a few settlers arrived in the area and set up a sawmill. Job

Carr, a Union army veteran, built a cabin in the area in 1864 and is considered Tacoma's first resident. When the railroad arrived in 1873, its terminal was about two miles from the settlement that had grown up around Carr's place, and the focus of development shifted there. But Tacoma did not really take off until it got a transcontinental railroad connection in 1883. Fires in 1884 and 1885 destroyed most of the city's wooden buildings, but Tacoma rebuilt itself with stone and brick, and many of those Victorian-era structures still stand. The **Job Carr Cabin Museum** (2350 North 30th St.; 253-627-5405) is a reconstruction completed in 2000.

Operated by the Washington State Historical Society, the **Washington State History Museum** (1911 Pacific Ave.; 253-272-3500) has extensive holdings focusing on the history of the state and the Pacific Northwest. Exhibits range from the history and culture of the region's various American Indian tribes to western expansion. The museum is one of six in the city's Museum District, but it is the only one covering the days of the Old West in and around Tacoma.

Judge **James L. Wickersham** (1857–1939), the jurist credited with bringing law and order to Alaska, moved to Washington Territory in 1883 and practiced law in Tacoma until he was appointed as Alaska's first federal district judge in 1900 (see Fairbanks and Juneau, Alaska). Wickersham, who later served five terms in Congress, spent the rest of his life in Alaska, but his remains were returned to Tacoma for burial in **Tacoma Cemetery** (4801 South Tacoma Way; 253-472-3369; Section 2J).

TOPPENISH (YAKIMA COUNTY)

Although not incorporated until 1907, Toppenish has kept the Wild West alive with a series of seventy-eight outdoor murals depicting the history of the area. The program began with an infusion of state seed money in 1989 during Washington's centennial celebration. A nonprofit organization called the Mural Society oversees the program and makes sure all murals are historically accurate. The public art project amounts to a visual history of rural Washington. A brochure listing all the murals and their location can be picked up at the Toppenish Mural Society's office (504 South Elm St., Tacoma; 509-865-6516), or is available online at visittoppenish.com.

Two miles north of town, the **Yakama Nation Cultural Center** (100 Spilyay Loop; 509-865-2800) is operated by the Yakama Nation and tells the story of the Yakama people and their culture.

Fort Simcoe (5150 Fort Simcoe Rd., White Swan; 509-874-2372) was established in 1856, during the Yakama War. Located near a series of springs the Yakama called *Mool* ("bubbling water"), the fort remained an active military post for just three years. When the army left in 1859, the property was conveyed to the Bureau of Indian Affairs and became the Indian agency for the Yakama Nation. The bureau also established a boarding school for Indian children with the intention of assimilating them to Euro-American ways.

The Yakama Nation leased the fort to the State of Washington in 1956 for use as a state historic park. Listed on the National Register of Historic Places, the old fort is located on the Yakama Indian Reservation. Five original post buildings still stand, three of which are open to the public. Other post structures have been reconstructed. An interpretive center has artifacts and exhibits telling the fort's story.

Appropriately housed in the 1911 Northern Pacific Railroad depot, the **Northern Pacific Railroad Museum** (10 South Asotin Ave.; 509-865-1911) details the history of the railroad. Opened in 1990, the museum includes a restored waiting room, telegraph office, and Railway Express Agency office, with vintage rolling stock on display outside.

VANCOUVER (CLARK COUNTY)

The first metropolis of the Pacific Northwest, Vancouver was named for British naval captain George Vancouver, who explored the area in 1792. Lewis and Clark camped in the vicinity in 1806, and the London-based Hudson's Bay Company opened a fortified fur-trading post here in 1825. The village that developed just west of the fort became the city of Vancouver.

Fort Vancouver, a square log stockade with blockhouses and cabins inside the protection of the walls, was constructed in 1825 and moved to a new site four years later. Twenty years after the British departed, fire destroyed the fort in 1866. Based on archaeological work done from 1947 to 1952, the fort was reconstructed by the National Park Service in the 1960s and opened as **Fort Vancouver National Historic Site** (612 East Reserve St.; 360-816-6230).

The US Army established a garrison on the bluff overlooking Hudson Bay in 1849 when the United States acquired the Oregon Territory. Variously known as Camp Vancouver, Columbia Barracks, Fort Vancouver, and **Vancouver Barracks**, the post remains active. Officers Row has twenty-one houses built from 1867 to 1906 for the post's officers. Two of the more noted quarters are the U. S. Grant House and the George C. Marshall House. While Marshall was a twentieth-century officer, numerous other notable military figures occupied the quarters over the years. Owned by the City of Vancouver, the **U. S. Grant House** (1101 Officers Row; 360-906-1101) and the **George C. Marshall House** (1301 E Evergreen Blvd.; 360-693-3103) are partially leased to private businesses.

The area's history is covered at the **Clark County Historical Museum** (1511 Main St.; 360-993-5679). The museum has standing and rotating exhibits, and the Clark County Historical Society's library has a large collection of archival material and photographs related to the Vancouver area. The museum and library occupy the former Carnegie Library, built in 1909.

WALLA WALLA (WALLA WALLA COUNTY)
This southeastern Washington town got its name courtesy of the explorers Lewis and Clark, who in 1805 noted that the native people with a village at the mouth of a small river that flowed into the Columbia called it *Wallah Wallah*—their term for "many waters." Lewis and Clark named the river and the people who lived there "Walla Walla."

A fur-trading post was later established in the vicinity of the village, but more than three decades would pass after Lewis and Clark's visit before settlement began in the area.

Whitman Massacre

In a way, Dr. Marcus Whitman, his wife Narcissa, and nearly a dozen others associated with Whitman's riverside mission in the Walla Walla Valley died of measles—but not of the disease itself. Whitman, his wife, and another couple traveled what would become the Oregon Trail in 1836 to establish a mission to minister to the Cayuse Indians. The Whitmans stayed in the valley while the other couple continued on to what would become Idaho Territory. As white settlers began arriving by the score, then hundreds and thousands in the mid-1840s, they brought their diseases with them. When measles broke out, about half the Indians in the area, including many children, died. The Whitmans and their fellows fared better, having some resistance to the disease.

But the Indians did not understand that. In retribution, on November 29, 1847, they killed Whitman and his wife and eleven others. Known as the **Whitman Massacre**, the incident marked the beginning of more than two decades of conflict in Washington and Oregon between American Indians, white settlers, and the US military.

The foundations of the mission structures are still visible at the **Whitman Mission National Historic Site** (328 Whitman Mission Rd.; 509-522-6360). A monument placed in 1897 marks the mass grave of the massacre victims.

The settlement of Walla Walla developed around the military post the army established seven miles west of the Whitman Mission site, in 1858. In the 1870s, soldiers at **Fort Walla Walla** participated in the Nez Perce and Bannock-Paiute wars. Well into the 1880s, Walla Walla was the largest city in Washington. The fort was abandoned in 1910. The **Fort Walla Walla Museum** (755 Myra Rd.; 509-525-7703) tells the story of the fort and the town.

Ferdinand J. "Ferd" Patterson, a professional gambler whose unsavory reputation preceded him, had only been in town a short time when he and Hugh Donahue had a run-in, which, as it developed, would keep Patterson in Walla Walla for the rest of his life—and beyond.

On February 15, 1866, Patterson was enjoying a shave inside Richard Bogel's barbershop when Donahue, a private cop in the employ of the local business community, walked in and warmed himself in front of the stove. The barber had just wiped the last of the lather off Patterson's face when Donahue raised a pistol and declared, "You must kill me or I'll kill you." Only Donahue didn't wait for Patterson to go for his gun, which hung on a nearby coat hook. Instead, he shot him in the jaw.

At that, Patterson jumped from the chair and ran toward the door as Donahue put a second bullet in him, missing with a third shot. The Irish rent-a-cop followed Patterson into an adjacent saloon and watched him fall to the floor. Then, just to make sure he was dead, he emptied his revolver into the man's body.

Arrested and tried for murder, Donahue saw the proceeding end in a mistrial, with seven jurors buying his attorney's self-defense argument while five voted to convict. Held in jail pending a second trial, Donahue walked out of an unlocked cell door, never to be seen again.

Patterson (1821–1866) is buried in **Walla Walla's Mountain View Cemetery** (2120 South Second Ave.; 509-527-4485). His round-top white marble tombstone does not stand out, except for the one word engraved beneath his name: "Assassinated." The barbershop stood at Third and Main Streets but later was razed.

YAKIMA (YAKIMA COUNTY)

Normally in the days of the Wild West, when railroad tracks were being laid in the direction of your town, that was very good news. Unfortunately for Yakima City, which had been settled on the Yakima River in the 1860s, the Northern Pacific Railroad decided in 1884 to establish a new town four miles north of the existing town. The new town would be called North Yakima.

After North Yakima had been platted, Yakima City residents were offered lots in the new town. Naturally, many businessmen and residents did not want to pull up stakes. Discord developed. The publisher of the *Yakima Signal* knew the town had to relocate or die, and he had the newspaper's frame building jacked up and readied for the move. One night, before that could happen, a Yakima City partisan dynamited the newspaper. Fortunately for the publisher, there was still enough lumber scattered around to make a good start on rebuilding in North Yakima.

The railroad finally agreed to pay for Yakima City's relocation, and the transition proceeded peacefully after that. Yakima City disappeared and the "North" was eventually dropped from the name of the new town, which boomed, as railroad towns did.

Established in 1952, the 65,000-square-foot **Yakima Valley Museum** (2105 Tieton Dr., Franklin Park; 509-248-0747) focuses on the natural and cultural history of the Yakima Valley, from its original inhabitants through the development of the town and county. The two-level museum has more than 48,000 artifacts. In addition to permanent and temporary exhibits, the museum also houses a large collection of books, documents, and photographs related to area history.

ALASKA

ANCHORAGE (ANCHORAGE BOROUGH)

The British explorer Captain James Cook did not discover the shorter water route between Europe and the Pacific Northwest that he sought, but as one of the first Europeans to map the Alaska coast, he came up with a place name for the area that would become the future US state's largest city. He called the place where for two weeks his ship *Resolute* lay at anchor "Anchor Point," a name later changed to Anchorage.

Cook may have provided some of Alaska's early place names, but it was Russia, not Great Britain, that came into possession of the huge land area in the late 1700s. That nation nominally controlled Alaska until selling it to the United States in 1867 for $7.2 million. The real estate deal had been put together by then secretary of state William Seward, and for a time it seemed like a wasteful expenditure of public funds. But a couple of years later, gold was discovered in the new US possession, and while the big boom would not come until late in the nineteenth century, it was soon evident that "Seward's Folly," as it was often called, had not been such a bad idea after all.

However, well into the second decade of the twentieth century—unlike the rest of the nation—Alaska had only a few miles of track laid by a railroad that had gone bankrupt. Appreciating the economic and military importance of a rail line, in 1914 President Woodrow Wilson signed the Alaska Railroad Act. The legislation created the Alaska Engineering Commission, tasked with building a railway that would connect the ice-free port of Seward with Fairbanks, a distance of five hundred miles. When AEC commissioner Frederick Mears arrived in 1915 to oversee the immense project, the commission established a construction camp at the mouth of Stickleback Creek (now known as Ship Creek) on Cook Inlet. Within a year the town had around three thousand residents.

The locale had long been a Dena'ina Athabascan fishing camp. In addition to these first inhabitants, men who had arrived from Central

Europe looking to land jobs as track layers had already set up a camp. Those men, in turn, attracted entrepreneurial women who would provide companionship, for a fee.

Not wanting a red-light district in the company town, the AEC, with help from the military, laid out a townsite away from the rough-and-tumble camp. Realizing that this would not shut down prostitution, the commission obligingly built a road from the newly platted Anchorage to the sin city site. And since the AEC considered the Central European men to be as undesirable as the working women, they also banned immigrant laborers from becoming Anchorage real estate owners.

Unfortunately for the business interests of the prostitutes, the US Forest Service—which managed the land on which the red-light district and immigrant tent camp had grown—were ordered in the summer of 1916 to clear the area, and federal workers tore down the brothels and crude residences they had built.

No governmental entity has ever completely done away with prostitution, but compared with most other railroad boomtowns in the West, Anchorage had better-than-average success in maintaining law and order and controlling vice. The community was incorporated in 1920, and three years later, the railroad project had been completed.

Anchorage grew to become Alaska's largest city. In fact, nearly half the state's residents live in the Anchorage metropolitan area today.

A log cabin with a sod roof, the **Anchorage Visitor Center** (4th Avenue and Avenue F; 907-257-2363) offers a glimpse of pioneer Alaskan architecture during the 1890s Klondike Gold Rush days.

While Alaska's wildest days were over by the time Anchorage grew to prominence, being the state's largest city, it also has the state's largest museum. The **Alaska Heritage Museum** (301 West Northern Lights; 907-265-2834) has exhibits on the turn-of-the-twentieth-century Gold Rush. It also has a collection focusing on the history of Wells Fargo, which played a vital role in getting newly mined gold to the Lower 48. The **Alaska Native Heritage Center** (8800 Heritage Center Dr.; 907-330-8000) focuses on the state's eleven major native cultures. The center was created in 1987 by the Alaska Federation of Natives and opened to the public in 1999.

Circle (Fairbanks Recording District)

Since the first discovery of gold in Alaska in 1873, American and Canadian prospectors who were hardy enough to put up with extreme cold, the midnight sun, scanty supplies, and all of the other difficulties associated with the remoteness of the northernmost US possession, looked for the next Mother Lode. When word spread that gold had been found in a Yukon River tributary known as Birch Creek, a party of Canadian miners rushed to the area to begin staking claims in 1893.

Soon, two rival companies had established log trading posts on the Yukon River about fifty miles from the new discovery. As other miners and those who would make money off them arrived, the community that developed was named Circle City, because it lay only fifty miles south of the Arctic Circle. In the summer months, the town—for a time referred to as the world's largest log city—was accessible by riverboat. Being a river port enhanced its status as a mining supply center, and it grew to a peak point of about seven hundred residents. The US Army established an infantry post in the vicinity in 1897. In addition to mercantile establishments and other businesses, the town at one point had a music hall, two theaters, eight dance halls, and twenty-eight saloons.

For a time, miners handled their own law enforcement, but in 1897 one of the West's more interesting characters arrived with a commission as a deputy US marshal. Everyone knew him as Frank M. Canton, but that was the alias Josiah W. "Joe" Horner had taken on to avoid apprehension for an 1877 bank robbery in Texas. He had turned straight, previously as a federal marshal having taken on the Doolin gang in Oklahoma, and participating as a hired gun in Wyoming's Johnson County War.

A newspaper article syndicated nationally in 1898 called Circle City "The future metropolis of the Klondike," but that assessment obviously had been predicated on the false belief that the gold supply in Alaska and the Yukon would not diminish. Canton decamped for a warmer clime in Oklahoma when this became evident, and so did most of its other residents. Still, the community managed to escape ghost-town status, even though "City" was dropped from its name long ago.

Though fire and time eliminated its Gold Rush–era architecture, Circle (162 miles northeast of Fairbanks on the Steese Highway) gets some tourist dollars from outdoor recreation enthusiasts. A mile southeast of town on an unpaved road along the Yukon River is **Pioneer Cemetery**, a one-acre site surrounded by forest that contains graves dating from the boomtown days. The nearby **Yukon–Charley Rivers National Preserve** is the town's biggest draw.

DAWSON CITY (YUKON TERRITORY, CANADA)

Though technically not in Alaska, Dawson City, Yukon Territory, is only sixty-six miles east of the Alaska state line–US border, and was the center of the Wild West's last great gold rush. As such, it had an impact not only on Alaska, but on the entire United States.

On August 16, 1896, George Washington Carmack, a Californian who had come to Alaska in 1885, a few years after deserting from the US Marine Corps, knelt to take a drink from Rabbit Creek, a stream that flowed into the Klondike River. As he did so, something shiny caught his eye. "I could see the raw gold laying thick between flaky slabs like cheese sandwiches," he recalled. "I felt as if I just dealt myself a royal flush in the game of life."

The find precipitated a small rush to the area, and the town of Dawson—named for Canadian geologist George Mercer Dawson—soon began to develop at the juncture of the Klondike and Yukon Rivers, about twenty miles from the site of the gold discovery. The fact that only about a thousand people descended on the area at first is only because the area was sparsely populated. But when Carmack showed up in Seattle a year later with roughly $3 million in gold, the news set off the great Klondike Gold Rush of 1897–1899. Soon, an estimated 100,000 men and some women headed "North to Alaska" (gold was being found both in Yukon Territory and the US side) to cash in on the bonanza. Which became the new name for Rabbit Creek: Bonanza Creek.

Dawson exploded from a community of five hundred or so to one that may have reached one hundred times that size before the boom ended. As with most boomtowns, population estimates varied, but the demographics were the same as with other Wild West boomtowns—all types, from miners to merchants to prostitutes and gamblers—showed up to capitalize on the sudden wealth coming from the streams and the earth. One of those who left the Lower 48 for the Yukon was long-haired, white-goateed Captain Jack Crawford, the so-called "Poet Scout of the West." Crawford had ridden with James Butler "Wild Bill" Hickok and Buffalo Bill Cody. Usually clad in his trademark buckskin shirt, Crawford operated a store he called the Wigwam, peddling everything from hay to ice cream.

Getting to the goldfields was a long, hard, and dangerous journey, and by the time most of the people wanting to cash in on the boom got there, all of the best ground had been claimed by the larger operators. On top of that, the duty the government of Canada imposed on gold ore made the economics impossible for all but the largest operators. Though relatively few people profited from it, an estimated $29 million in gold was extracted before the lode diminished below the level of profitability. The Klondike Gold Rush is credited with ending the US economic depression of the mid-1890s, the most severe financial crisis the nation would face until the twentieth century's Great Depression.

The **Dawson City Museum** (595 Fifth Ave.; 867-993-5291) is located in the Old Territorial Administration Building, built between 1899 and 1901. The museum's exhibits cover the area's natural and cultural history, with particular emphasis on the Gold Rush days. A young writer named Jack London from California, who would become world-famous for his classic novel *A Call of the Wild*, was drawn to the Yukon during the Gold Rush and spent the winter of

1897 in Dawson City. The **Jack London Museum** (600 Firth St.; 867-993-5575) focuses on this writer's colorful, if short, life.

One of the Old West's most unusual historic sites is known as the **Paddlewheel Graveyard,** something of a Boot Hill for many of the riverboats that once plied the Klondike and Yukon Rivers. Given the remoteness of Dawson, the riverboat era lasted longer on these two rivers than anywhere else in the West. But the development of roads into the region in the 1950s finally beached the industry—and many of the boats. Boats left moored along the river over the years were left high and dry by flooding, and they began to fall apart. To reach the "graveyard," take the George Black Ferry from the north end of Front Street to the other side of the Yukon. From the Yukon River Campground, walk along a trail for about an eighth of a mile to the area of accumulated wreckage. The site is not managed, and the Dawson City website urges visitors to be "bear-aware."

DYEA (BOROUGH OF SKAGWAY)

Two Alaskan towns flourished as gateways during the Klondike Gold Rush—Dyea and Skagway—but only Skagway survived.

Located where the Taiya River and Taiya Inlet meet, south of Chilkoot Pass, Dyea was only six miles from Skagway. But each town connected to a different route to reach the goldfields. From Dyea, prospectors and others hoping to make their fortune took the Chilkoot Trail. From Skagway, men and women bound for the Yukon traveled the White Pass Trail (see Skagway).

While each town was an embarkation point to the Yukon, Dyea was somewhat disadvantaged in that it was only a shallow-water port. Skagway, however, could accommodate larger, deeper-draft vessels. Even so, for a time Dyea was one of the most important communities in Alaska, boasting several scores of businesses. Elements of the Fourteenth Infantry established Camp Dyea there in 1898, one of eleven military posts active in Alaska during the Gold Rush. When the White Pass and Yukon Railroad opted to lay tracks along the White Pass Trail rather than using the Chilkoot route, it was a death sentence for Dyea and life-saving for Skagway. The soldiers marched off in 1899, and Dyea rapidly lost much of its population.

"There is no longer a port of Dyea," the *Klondike Nugget* in Dawson City reported on June 10, 1900. "The erstwhile busy town having lost its teeming population of hurrying gold seekers and temporary traders and dwellers, has lapsed into a deep sleep. . . . The thousands of former townsfolk [have] dwindled to hundreds, and the hundreds to a few tens."

Today, only one wood-frame building dating from the community's heyday still stands. But there are numerous foundations and scattered remnants of building material dating from the boom days. What's left of the town's wharf is also visible. Two cemeteries accommodate the remains of those who never left Dyea. The most interesting burial ground is the **Slide Cemetery**, where most of the grave markers show the same day of death—April 3, 1898. On that day, Palm Sunday, an avalanche on the Chilkoot Trail killed anywhere from sixty-three to one hundred gold seekers and others on their way to the Klondike. The once-thriving townsite is a National Historic Landmark and part of the **Klondike Gold Rush National Historical Park**.

EAGLE (SOUTHEAST FAIRBANKS CENSUS AREA)

A trading post known as Belle Isle opened in 1874 on the Yukon River near the Canadian border in the vicinity of the future town of Eagle. When the Klondike Gold Rush began in 1897, Eagle took flight as a supply and trade center for miners and soon reached its peak population of 1,700-plus. The local economy got a further boost in 1899 when the US Army established Fort Egbert on a rocky bluff overlooking the town, which became the first incorporated city in the Alaska interior in 1901.

The **Eagle Historical Society and Museum** (Third Ave., Eagle National Historic District; 907-547-2325) includes eight restored historic buildings dating from the Gold Rush days: four buildings that were part of **Fort Egbert**, which was abandoned in 1911; the log structure that housed the Improved Order of Red Men Lodge; the US Custom House; the old federal courthouse; and a two-story frame building where noted jurist James Wickersham (see Fairbanks) had his district court before he moved it to Fairbanks when Eagle declined after the Yukon gold boom went bust.

FAIRBANKS (FAIRBANKS NORTH STAR BOROUGH)

Alaska's last gold boomtown, Fairbanks, dates to 1901, when transplanted Ohioan E. T. Barnette opened a trading post at a high point above the Chena River.

With $20,000 in inventory shipped from San Francisco, Barnette's intention was to establish his business on the Tanana River at a point called the Tanana Crossing, well upstream from the Chena. Providentially, low water kept the 150-foot steamboat he had chartered from going that far upriver. Unable to go farther, the captain of the sternwheeler *Lavelle Young* turned around and made for where the Chena River met the Tanana. Barnette intended to wait there until the spring thaw had raised the level of the Tanana, at which point he'd resume his journey to Tanana Crossing. The following year, however, prospector Felix Pedro discovered gold in nearby Fish Creek, and another rush—Alaskans called them stampedes—was on. Barnette was sitting pretty where he was, and a new town had been born. Following Fairbanks' incorporation in 1903, Barnette was elected its first mayor.

For insight into Fairbanks and its gold-mining history, visit the **Fairbanks Community Museum** (535 Second Ave.; 907-457-3669) and the **Alaska Mining Hall of Fame Museum** (825 First Ave.; 907-456-1933). Located in the 1905-vintage bath house and Odd Fellows Hall, the museum opened in 2014. Another gold-mining-related venue is **Gold Dredge No. 8 National Historic Site** (1803 Old Steese Highway; 907-479-6673).

The Law West of the Yukon

Illinois-born James L. Wickersham (1857–1939) came to Alaska in 1900 from Tacoma, Washington, to restore law and order in America's last frontier. But he would do his work cloaked in a judicial robe and wielding a gavel, not wearing a badge and gun. Appointed by President William McKinley to the newly created Third Judicial District, Wickersham arrived at age forty-three with his wife and son to set up court in Eagle City, on the Yukon River. Later, he moved the court—which handled both civil and criminal cases—to newly founded Fairbanks (which he had suggested be named for Charles W. Fairbanks, later vice president under Theodore Roosevelt).

As a federal judge with jurisdiction over 300,000 square miles of interior Alaska, Wickersham spent the next eight years presiding over cases involving mining claim disputes, public corruption, jury fixing, and other matters. In addition to the legal verbiage entered into his written orders and docket books, he faithfully kept a personal journal that often told the real story, including this description of a less-than-honorable individual who came to his judicial notice: "I am satisfied that he is, to use a mining camp expression, 'so crooked that his blood only circulates once a year.'"

The small frame house Judge Wickersham built in 1904 at the corner of First Avenue and Noble Street in Fairbanks, and lived in until he moved to Juneau, has been restored and now stands in **Pioneer Park** (2500 Airport Way; 907-586-9001). The forty-acre park opened in 1967 at the Alaska '67 Centennial Exposition, in celebration of the hundredth anniversary of the United States' purchase of Alaska from Russia.

HAINES (BOROUGH OF HAINES)

Located south of Skagway and north of Juneau on a peninsula that juts into the Lynn Canal fjord, Haines developed in the late 1870s as a trading post near the site of a Chilkat village. In 1881 a Presbyterian mission was opened nearby, and the town that developed around it was named for Mrs. F. E. Haines, the woman who helped raise money for the mission. A cannery operated there, and in the late 1890s the town benefited from the Klondike Gold Rush and a later discovery closer to the community, which grew as a mining center. In 1898 the US Army established **Fort William H. Seward** just outside of Haines, and the post continued in operation until the end of World War II.

Completed in 1904, the fort—named for the man who as US secretary of state negotiated the purchase of Alaska from Russia—is a collection of eighty-five mostly well-preserved Victorian-era buildings, considered one of the state's top historic sites.

Haines's story is told at the **Haines Sheldon Museum** (11 Main St.; 907-766-2366). Located on the grounds of the old mission, the museum's extensive holdings range from Chilkat artifacts to a sizable archival collection of everything from old ship's logs to mining journals.

JUNEAU (BOROUGH OF JUNEAU)

Joseph Juneau spent most of his life in quest of gold. His first experience as a prospector came in 1849, when the sixteen-year-old French-Canadian traveled to the goldfields of Northern California. From there he went to Oregon when gold excitement held sway there, and after that boom played out, he headed for British Columbia during another gold rush. To get there, he traveled through Wrangell, Alaska, his first visit to the future state.

In 1879, Sitka, Alaska–based mining engineer George Pilz, a German immigrant, hired Juneau and Richard Harris to search for gold in southeastern Alaska. With a native Alaskan named Kowee as their guide, the two men found placer gold in a tributary of Alaska's Gastineau Channel. That stream, soon dubbed Gold Creek, netted them a thousand pounds of gold nuggets and dust.

The city of Juneau grew from Harris and Juneau's mining camp, first called Harrisburg, and then Rockwell. At a meeting of miners on December 14, 1881, someone suggested the growing community be named Pilzburg for the man who thought to explore the area for gold, but when the matter came to a vote, Juneau received forty-seven votes, with twenty-one miners preferring Harrisburg, and only four liking Rockwell. This vote would seem a perfect example of the democratic process, but Joseph Juneau is said to have offered free drinks to the electorate in exchange for their vote. Another version of the story has Juneau buying drinks for all *after* the election.

Despite early favorable indications, production around Juneau never compared with the later Klondike bonanza and other precious metal–inspired stampedes, but Juneau became an important waypoint for in-bound gold seekers and the supplies they needed. In addition to being a port, Juneau was designated as the territorial capital in 1906, and would remain Alaska's largest city well into the twentieth century.

Joseph Juneau (1836–1899) took part in one last boom, this time as a restaurateur in Dawson, Yukon Territory. That's where he died, but in 1903 his remains were returned to the city that bears his name. He lies beneath a weathered concrete slab in **Evergreen Cemetery** (601 Seater St.; 907-364-2828). An oxidized metal plaque with a bas-relief of mountains and deciduous trees notes his name, dates of birth and death, and bears this legend: "Co-Founder of the City of Juneau." Illustrative of how Alaskans would view gold for posterity, Evergreen Cemetery was established in 1887 to replace the community's original cemetery on a prominence known as Chicken Ridge. Where bodies had once been buried, gold would soon be mined.

The Earp Files

In 2018, the **Alaska State Library, Archives and Museum** (395 Whittier St.; 907-465-2920) completed the digitization of all records it has pertaining to gambler-gunman Wyatt Earp's time in Alaska during the Klondike Gold Rush, including the liquor license he and his business partner obtained for his saloon in Nome and other legal papers related to Earp's occasional run-ins with the law while in Alaska. The records show that Earp paid $1,500 for his license to sell "intoxicating liquors" at his Dexter Saloon in Nome. That amount of money had the buying power of more than $50,000 today. While the state library and museum focuses on all of Alaska's history, the **Juneau–Douglas City Museum** (4th and Main Streets; 907-465-2920) spotlights the city's history.

Opened in 1950 in a much older building, the **Red Dog Saloon** (278 South Franklin St.; 907-463-3658) has been recognized by the Alaska legislature as the oldest man-made tourist attraction in Juneau. Wyatt Earp never hoisted a brew at the Red Dog, but the watering hole does display an interesting relic reputedly associated with him. Hanging behind the saloon's bar is a framed Smith & Wesson Model 3 revolver; manufactured between 1870 and 1915, the pistols were variously chambered from .32 to .44 caliber, although the caliber of the supposed Earp gun has not been reported. Accompanying the gun is this explanatory verbiage:

C-H-E-C-K-E-D but never claimed. This weapon was checked at the U.S. Marshal's office in Juneau, June 27, 1900, by the notorious gunfighter WYATT EARP. Earp departed for Nome aboard the S.S. Senator at 5:00 a.m. on June 29th prior to the opening of the Marshal's office.

That's a great story, but in the summer of 2018 a reporter for Alaska Public Media in Juneau could find no records supporting any connection between the Red Dog firearm and Earp. In fact, the journalist discovered a contemporary article in the *Nome Daily News* reporting that Earp had been arrested in Nome on June 29, 1900, following a barroom brawl. Since Nome is 1,096 miles from Juneau as the horned puffin flies, that rips a glacier-sized hole in the claim that Earp sailed from Juneau on June 29, 1900, and left a pistol behind.

"The Shooting of Dan McGrew"

Called the bard of the Yukon, Canadian poet Robert W. Service (1874–1958) early on grasped the oft-cited advice that if you're going to be a writer, you better have a day job. Accordingly, he made his living as a clerk at the Canadian Bank of Commerce in Victoria, British Columbia, and wrote his poems on his own time. In 1904, on his way to a new position with his bank's Whitehorse branch in gold-rich Yukon Territory, Service laid over in Juneau for a few days. There, the story goes, the English-born gent wandered into a bar called The Missouri and ended up witnessing a gunfight. That affray supposedly became the basis for Service's classic poem, "The Shooting of Dan McGrew."

The Missouri is no longer around, but the site is now occupied by the **Imperial Saloon** (241 Front St.; 907-586-1960). Opened in 1891, it is the oldest bar in Alaska. One more thing about Service and Alaska: The poet characterized those who were drawn to the then-territory as "a race of men who don't fit in."

Judge James Wickersham (see Fairbanks) spent the last years of his life in Juneau, living in a Victorian house at 213 7th Street until his death in 1928. The house is a state historic site.

NOME (UNORGANIZED BOROUGH OF ALASKA)

Nearer Moscow (4,032 miles) than Miami (4,475 miles), Nome lies only 143 miles south of the Arctic Circle in northwestern Alaska. Truly, it stands as the northernmost outpost of the Wild West. But its remoteness made no difference when gold was discovered in and around there in 1898. The real boom came a year later when gold deposits were found in astounding quantity on the beach along which Nome had developed.

Among the thousands of men and women who descended on Nome intent on panning for gold or mining the prospectors of their hard-earned money was the legendary Wyatt Earp of O.K. Corral fame. Partnering with Charles Hoxie, Earp and his common-law wife Josie built a two-story frame saloon on rowdy Front Street. They called it the Dexter Saloon, and it made them rich for a time. Not only did Earp sell booze, run a gambling operation, and offer for-hire female companionship upstairs, but his business also became a gathering place that amounted to a town hall and community center. Though Earp did well financially, his overblown reputation took a hit when he got carried away one night, pulled a pistol, and announced, "That's how we do it down Arizona way!" Deputy US Marshal Albert J. Lowe slapped Earp, disarmed him, and said, "That's how we do it in Alaska!" The federal lawman told him to go home and sleep it off, and that he could reclaim his six-shooter in the morning. (Although the story sounds apocryphal, Lowe *was* the deputy marshal in Nome at the time.)

The Earps spent portions of four years in Alaska, returning to California during the winters. They made a fortune, but that money proved as ephemeral as the gold rush itself.

Two other noted characters spent time in Nome—former Tombstone, Arizona, mayor and newspaper publisher John Clum, who worked as a US postal inspector in Nome and was later appointed postmaster in Fairbanks, and former Texas cowboy George Lewis "Tex" Rickard. "Tex" had gone bust in the Yukon before coming to Nome to try his luck. Opting to go for coin and cash rather than gold itself, the Texan opened the Northern Saloon. Rickard and Earp were friendly competitors and enlivened Nome's dark winter months with boxing bouts they organized. Rickard would become a millionaire, but not in Nome. When the boom faded, he returned to the Lower 48. In New York, he built the third Madison Square Garden, founded the New York Rangers hockey team, and got rich as a boxing promoter.

Nome later suffered two catastrophic fires and five devastating Bering Sea storms. Consequently, very little of the city's gold-rush-era Victorian architecture remains. Earp's Dexter Saloon, long gone, was located where Nome's City Hall is now. A sign there gives an overview of the saloon, noting that it stood twenty feet to the northwest. Next to the sign is a bronze marker pointing out that this area once was Nome's red-light district.

Still standing within an easy walk of the Dexter site is the old Discovery Saloon at 1st and D Streets. Now a private residence, this two-story wood-frame building with a false front was built in 1901 by Max Gordon, who operated a tony public establishment on the premises. It is the oldest onetime commercial building in Nome, and one of the few surviving structures dating to the gold rush days. The building was listed on the National Register of Historic Places in 1980. The **Carrie M. McLain Memorial Museum** (100 West 7th Ave., inside the Richard Foster Building) has exhibits on the gold-boom days as well as artifacts from the Dexter Saloon.

St. Michael (Nome Census Area)

Originally an Inuit village, St. Michael is named for Redoubt St. Michael, a fortified trading post established there by the Russian-American Company in 1833. One hundred twenty-four miles across Norton Sound from Nome, the now-small community boomed during the 1897 Klondike Gold Rush, boasting a short-lived population of as many as ten thousand people. To help maintain order, the US Army established **Fort St. Michael** there.

Back in Alaska for the second time, Wyatt and Josie Earp caught a riverboat in St. Michael bound for the Klondike, but the vessel got trapped in ice. They were rescued and taken back to St. Michael, where they spent the rest of the winter before finally getting to Nome. While in St. Michael, the Earps became acquainted with novelist Rex Beach, a young writer named Jack London, Tex Rickard, and Charlie Hoxie, a prominent bootlegger. The cabin the Earps are said to have stayed in that winter still stands, but is privately owned.

Even following the Gold Rush, St. Michael remained an important shipping point until the opening of the Alaska Railroad. Most of its residents today are Yup'ik Eskimo. Many others are descendants of Russian traders.

SITKA (BOROUGH OF SITKA)

The first people to live on the west coast of Baranof Island on Sitka Sound were the Tlingits, who called their village "Shee Atika." Russians exploring the Pacific Coast first noted the location in 1741, but more than a half-century would pass before the Russian-American Company established a fortified trading post there, called St. Michael's Redoubt. The Russian community that grew around it was called "New Archangel."

Tlingit tribesmen attacked the fort in 1802, emptying its warehouse of trade goods before putting the log outpost to the torch. Two years later, the Russian navy violently reclaimed the site, destroying a Tlingit fortification. By 1808, the Tlingits having vacated the area, Sitka became the capital of Russian Alaska.

The Russian presence in North America ended with the purchase of Alaska by the United States in 1867. On October 18 of that year, on a rocky prominence overlooking the bay, the Russian flag came down as artillery pieces of both nations fired a salute. Then, amid continuing cannon fire, the Stars and Stripes went up over the new US possession, a huge land acquisition second in size only to the Louisiana Purchase of 1803.

Following the US acquisition of Alaska, Sitka prospered as a major seaport, exporting furs, salmon, lumber, and ice to California, Mexico, Hawaii, and Asia. It remained the capital of Alaska until 1906, when the seat of government was relocated to Juneau. Today, Sitka is a popular port of call for cruise ships.

Castle Hill (Harbor Rd. and Lincoln St.) is the site of the original Russian fortification, the place where the Russian flag was lowered and the American flag raised when the United States took possession of Alaska. Nothing remains of the fort, but in 1965 the state parks department built a stone parapet on the spot (now an Alaskan state park) and six eighteenth-century Russian cannons were positioned to overlook the bay. Nearby is a replica of one of the Russian-built wooden blockhouses that were part of the original redoubt's defenses.

Completed in 1843, the two-story **Russian Bishop's House** (501 Lincoln St.; 907-747-0110) served as the residence of Ivan Veniaminov, the first bishop of Alaska. A National Historic Landmark and part of **Sitka National Historical Park** (103 Monastery St.), the bishop's house is one of the oldest surviving buildings dating to the time of Russia's presence in Alaska.

The **Sheldon Jackson Museum** (104 College Dr.; 907-747-8981) and the **Southeast Alaskan Indian Cultural Center** (106 Metlakatla St.) focus on the history and culture of the native peoples of the Sitka area. Operated by the Sitka Historical Society, the **Sitka History Museum** (330 Harbor Dr.; 907-738-3766) has 8,000 artifacts, hundreds of paintings, 25,000 historic photographs, and 100,000 archival documents

SKAGWAY (BOROUGH OF SKAGWAY)

Native Tlingits called it Skagua, "the place where the north wind blows." Captain William Moore, the first nonnative settler, arrived in 1887, but the coastal town at the head of Taiya Inlet dates from the summer of 1897, when prospectors streamed in during the Klondike boom. Thousands of gold seekers followed the forty-mile White Pass Trail from Skagway to Lake Bennett and then by boat down the Yukon River for five hundred miles to the diggings around Dawson, in the Yukon Territory. Gold seekers also could take the slightly shorter but much harder Chilkoot Trail that began at nearby Dyea. The familiar alchemy of potential wealth mixed with an influx of people to an isolated area transformed Skagway into a thriving gateway city of tents and frame buildings. Soon Skagway was Alaska's second-largest city, but the rule of law was only a concept. When the boom played out in 1900, a rail connection kept it from becoming a ghost town. Today, it is a popular cruise ship destination.

Soapy Smith: Scammin' Scamp

There's no telling what Georgia-born Jefferson Randolph "Soapy" Smith could have accomplished in life if he had chosen to use his creative genius in more wholesome ways. A con artist who followed gold rush money from Colorado to Skagway, one of his purported if hard to believe scams involved opening a phony telegraph office with no connection whatsoever to the outside world. As the story goes, one of the fake telegraphers in his employ bilked gold miners of their money by charging them $5 per never-sent message. Then, based on information gleaned from their initial wire, senders received a bogus telegram (collect, of course) notifying them of a dire need to wire money to cover some family emergency. The cash paid for money orders went into Smith's pocket as well. In addition to that alleged scam, Smith supposedly ran a freight operation that never delivered anything.

When the Spanish-American War broke out, the legend is that Smith even set up a phony enlistment station where patriotic volunteers got their clothing and other possessions stolen after disrobing so a fake doctor could give them a physical. Later scholarship shows that Smith might not have been as big a crime boss in Skagway as the media has portrayed him to be, but he was no church deacon. He ran crooked games and assorted scams while trying to build an image as a generous civic leader, keeping his hands clean by practicing the management technique of delegation. His men, known as the Soap Gang, met new arrivals at the docks posing variously as newspaper reporters, preachers, and freighters or simply as savvy locals more than happy to help a stranger. If they determined someone had money, they steered him to whatever scam they felt he would be most susceptible to. That, or they singled him out for the more traditional form of robbery.

When members of Soapy Smith's gang relieved a well-thought-of miner of more than $2,600 in gold dust and cash, the good people of Skagway decided they'd had enough of the shifty grifter. An already-established, quasi-governmental body known as the Committee of 101 intended to clean up the town. On July

8, 1898, when Smith tried to crash a meeting of the pro-law-and-order group, the thirty-eight-year-old criminal genius died in a gunfight on the Juneau wharf. City engineer Frank Reid, one of the law-and-order men, suffered a mortal wound in the shoot-out and died twelve days later. However, some witnesses said that while Reid had been a major player in the fight, someone else may have fired the shot that killed Smith. Either way, Smith would no longer be scamming folks.

Erected in 1998, a bronze plaque on the southeast corner of Second Avenue and State Street in Skagway marks the site of the Smith–Reid gunfight. The marker says the gunfight took place on Sylvester's Wharf, but it actually happened on the Juneau Company Wharf.

While all of Skagway is included in the **Skagway and White Pass National Historic Landmark,** the historic heart of the city is its business district. Property ownership is both public and private, but all the historic structures—around a hundred buildings—are protected by law.

The modest structure on Sixth Avenue that served both as saloon and headquarters for Soapy Smith's decidedly immodest criminal enterprises still stands, albeit at a different location. After Smith's violent demise, the wooden, false-front building—a bank before Smith bought it—became a restaurant, and later saw use as a fire department garage. Local tourism promoter Martin Itjen bought the building in 1935 and transformed it into what he called **Jeff. Smiths Parlor** (maybe there wasn't enough room on the sign to spell out "Jefferson"). When Itjen died in 1942, his friend and gold rush memorabilia collector George Rapuzzi acquired the building and moved it to its current location. Following Rapuzzi's death in 1986, the structure fell into disrepair until a nonprofit foundation acquired it and four other historic Skagway buildings and gave them to the National Park Service. Following extensive restoration, the NPS reopened the nineteen-by-forty-foot building as a museum, in 2018 (Second Avenue between Broadway and State Streets).

The **Klondike Gold Rush National Historical Park** visitor center in the old White Pass and Yukon Railway depot (Second Avenue and Broadway; 907-983-9200) features Gold Rush exhibits and regular showings of a film on the Gold Rush and area history. Park rangers offer special programs and lead walking tours along historic Broadway in the summer. The two-story wood-frame WP&Y depot was built in 1898. The park has a number of historic structures, including the 1887 Captain William Moore Cabin, the 1898 Mascot Saloon, and an early rescue mission.

Located in the 1899-vintage Arctic Brotherhood Hall, the **Trail of '98 Museum** (700 Spring St., City Hall; 907-983-2420) is said to be the most photographed building in Alaska. Added in 1900, the mosaic covering the building's false front is made up of more than 8,800 pieces of driftwood from Skagway beaches.

Skagway's first burial occurred in the **Gold Rush Cemetery** in 1898. For the most part, the cemetery was no longer used after 1908. One hundred and forty-one graves are known in the cemetery, but the two most famous burial sites are those of Soapy Smith and Frank Reid. Smith's tombstone, his fifth, is plain and to the point, recording only his name (but not his famous nickname), birth and death dates, and his age of thirty-eight. The epitaph on Reid's gravestone, the cemetery's largest, reads: "He gave his life for the honor of Skagway."

Take Main Street north to 23rd Avenue and the railroad yards. Cross 23rd and follow the gravel road around and behind the railroad yards, crossing the tracks. The cemetery is located on a hillside in the nearby woods, just west of town.

A Monument for Mollie and One for the Missus

Many women flocking to Alaska during the Gold Rush were soiled doves, but not redheaded Mollie Walsh. Reaching Skagway in

1897, she wanted to make money, but not as a prostitute. Active in her church, she ran a grub tent on the White Pass Trail about thirty miles from Skagway, and became famous both for her cooking (particularly her pies) and her caring nature.

Two packers, men who made their living hauling supplies on the trail, soon vied for her hand in marriage, and Mike Bartlett won out over Jack Newman. The couple did well financially in Skagway and later in Dawson, but Bartlett drank heavily and abused Mollie. Taking their young son, Mollie left her husband and went to Seattle. Bartlett found her and shot her dead, on October 27, 1902, in the alley behind the boardinghouse where she was staying. Found innocent by reason of insanity, Bartlett later killed himself. Newman also settled in Seattle, where he married and enjoyed a successful business career. But he never forgot Mollie, and in 1930 commissioned a bronze sculpture of her and had it placed in Skagway. The inscription reads:

> ALONE WITHOUT HELP / THIS COURAGEOUS GIRL / RAN A GRUB TENT / DURING THE GOLD RUSH OF 1897–1898. / SHE FED AND LODGED / THE WILDEST GOLD CRAZED MEN. / GENER-ATIONS SHALL SURELY KNOW / THIS INSPIR-ING SPIRIT. / MURDERED OCT. 27, 1902.

Unable to attend the dedication, he wired: "I'm an old man and no longer suited to the scene, for Mollie is still young and will remain forever young, her spirit fingers still reach across the years and play on the slackened strings of my old heart and my heart still sings—MOLLIE! . . . but in such sad undertone that none but God and I can hear."

Touching as Newman's sentiments were, his wife Hannah was not keen on her husband's lasting tribute to a lost love. Moving fast, Newman had a bronze relief of Mrs. Newman made. That inscription read:

> MRS. HANNAH NEWMAN / WITH COURAGE AND FAITH IN THE DEVELOPMENT OF OUR

CITY OWNED / THIS GROUND FROM PIONEER
DAYS / UNTIL THE ERECTION OF THIS BUILD-
ING / 1930.

Newman died the following year. Although he had requested
that he be laid to rest beside Mollie's monument, Mrs. Newman
had him buried in Seattle. The monument stands in Mollie Walsh
Park, off 6th Avenue east of Broadway. The plaque honoring Mrs.
Newman is located outside the Washington Athletic Club, Sixth
and Union Streets, in Seattle.

VALDEZ (CHUGACH CENSUS AREA)

Named for eighteenth-century Spanish naval officer Antonio Valdez y
Basan, Valdez was born during the Alaskan gold rush of what was
essentially a scam.

When word of the Yukon gold discovery reached Seattle, the
reaction to the news was almost universal: How can I—or we—get
rich? The Pacific Steam Whaling Company—which operated a
trading post at the small port of Valdez and had a cannery at what is
now Cordova, Alaska—began promoting what it touted as a shorter
land route from Valdez to the goldfields. Calling it the "All-America
Route" from Valdez to the interior via the Valdez Glacier and Klutina
River, the company soon was joined in the scheme by outfitters and
newspapers eager for advertising revenue. Newspapers and outfitters
collaborated in the advertisement of this route. While there was such
a route, it was much more arduous than advertised. In fact, many a
would-be miner died after falling for the scam.

Ethics aside, what was good for the whaling company was good
for Valdez, which by the early spring of 1898 was a tent city with
roughly eight hundred residents.

Valdez survived the end of the Gold Rush, but not the tsunami
caused by the deadly 1964 Alaskan earthquake. The disaster destroyed
the old town and resulted in a new townsite on higher ground.

Despite the loss of any structures dating to the Gold Rush era, a collection of artifacts from Valdez's boom days survived, and is curated at the **Valdez Museum** (217 Egan Dr.; 907-835-2764).

Credit for that is due to a prospector named Joseph Bourke, who in 1901 put on display assorted "curiosities." The collection, which grew over time, was displayed in various buildings until the earthquake.

During the 1967 observance of the one hundredth anniversary of the Alaskan purchase, a state grant funded a museum building. Another grant in 1976 during the American bicentennial celebration paid for renovation and expansion of the building. What's known as the Egan Commons was developed adjacent to the building in 1989.

WRANGELL (BOROUGH OF WRANGELL)

Though long home to the Stikine Tlingit people, the island town of Wrangell dates to 1834, when Alaska was Russian territory. Concerned by the Hudson's Bay Company's reported interest in extending their fur trapping to the Stikine River, Governor Baron Ferdinand Petrovich von Wrangell ordered the construction of a fortification to block British access to the river.

Arriving in two ships, a contingent of soldiers built a wooden stockade with blockhouses called Redoubt St. Dionysius, and positioned artillery there. That summer, when the sails of a Hudson's Bay Company ship appeared on an obvious course for the mouth of the river, warning shots from the fort changed the mind of the vessel's captain, and British encroachment aspirations were checked for the time being. When Russia sold Alaska to the United States in 1867, American troops arrived to occupy the post, which they called **Fort Wrangell**. Two years later, troops stationed there would unleash an artillery barrage not as an act of war, but to resolve a law enforcement issue.

On Christmas night 1869, post quartermaster Sergeant Jacob Muller hosted a party at his residence. In the spirit of the season, the sergeant invited people from the nearby Stikine village, as well as his military comrades. Speaking of spirits, contrary to military regulation, they flowed freely at the gathering. At some point, a Stikine man known as Lowan began fighting with his wife and Mrs. Sergeant Muller stepped in to stop it. In response, Lowan bit off one of the woman's fingers. Then, his battered wife in tow, he fled from the fort.

Soon a squad of soldiers descended on the village to arrest him. In violently resisting, Lowan was shot and killed by one of the soldiers. The following morning, Lowan's father Sculd-doo showed up at the fort bent on revenge. Encountering post trader Leon Smith outside the walls of the fort, Sculd-doo shot him several times, leaving him mortally wounded. Then Sculd-doo returned to his village, as his son had done the night before. The ranking officer sent a message to the village demanding Sculd-doo's surrender by noon that day. If not, the commander threatened, he would train his six-pounder on the village and open fire. The officer's order was ignored, and when the deadline passed, he ordered his gunners to commence firing. With artillery rounds raining down on the village, the native people began firing their muskets toward the fort and made an unsuccessful attempt to capture the field piece.

The following day, the post's commander ordered that exploding shells from the detachment's twelve-pound howitzer be rained down on the village. More skirmishing followed, but the village finally released Sculd-doo. Tried before a military court on December 28, Sculd-doo, who said he had only been abiding by tribal law in getting retribution for his son's death, was found guilty of murder, and sentenced to death. He was hanged the next day.

The army abandoned the fort in 1870, but reactivated it in 1875 to maintain order during the Cassiar gold rush. The fort was shuttered again two years later, and its buildings sold at auction.

The gold rush of the early 1870s was nothing compared with the stampede that followed the discovery of gold in the Yukon in 1897. Many of the gold seekers who passed through Wrangell on their way to the Klondike, along with those who hoped to cash in on the boom in other ways, engaged in enough rowdy behavior to earn Wrangell its reputation as a "hell on wheels" town. Among the new arrivals was a tall man and his wife who most recently had lived in San Diego, California. His name was Wyatt Earp and his wife was Josie.

Having run out of money before reaching the bonanza country, Earp took a temporary job as a deputy marshal. He stayed on the payroll for only ten days before the man who would assume the duties on a more permanent basis arrived. Earp may have corralled a few drunks, but he had no Gunfight-at-the-O.K.-Corral moment in Wrangell. Decades later, after Earp had achieved Wild West icon status, promoters looking for ways to sell Wrangell began pointing out that their town had been the last place Earp ever worked as a lawman. Though he left when the job ended, not because the position had been challenging, someone with a penchant for alliteration pronounced that Wrangell had been "Too wild for Wyatt."

The city-owned **Wrangell Museum** (296 Campbell Dr.; 907-874-3770) chronicles Wrangell's past, from its native Tlingit heritage through the Klondike Gold Rush.

INDEX

ABOUT THE AUTHOR

An elected member of the Texas Institute of Letters, **Mike Cox** is the author of more than thirty-five nonfiction books. Over an award-winning freelance career dating back to his high school days, he has written hundreds of newspaper articles and columns, magazine stories, and essays for a wide variety of regional and national publications. When not writing, he spends as much time as he can traveling, fishing, hunting, and looking for new stories to tell. He lives in the Hill Country village of Wimberley, Texas.

To learn more about the author and his work, visit mikecoxauthor .com.